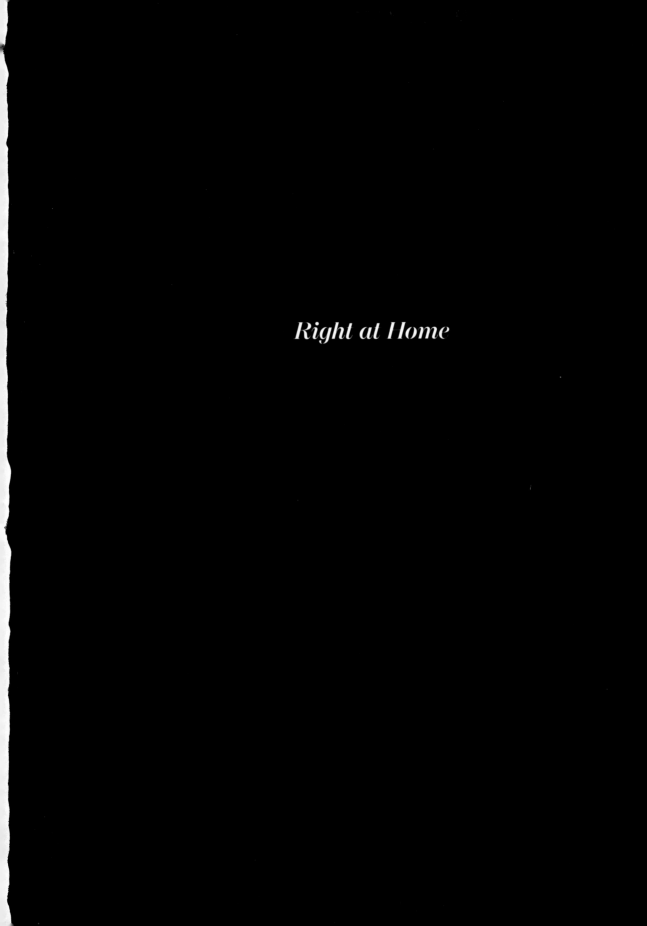

Right at Home

Right at Home

*How Good Design
Is Good for the Mind*

Bobby Berk

with Jamie Park

Clarkson Potter/Publishers
New York

To YOU.

You have helped support and lift me up over the years. Now my hope is that, in return, these pages will help you to create a space that not only you are proud of but also betters your own life with every moment you spend in it.

Contents

Introduction

The way your home makes you feel matters.

The first time I knew design had the power to transform my mind, I was five years old.

Inspired by the cool, blue tones from a dinosaur poster I had found at a local arts and crafts store, I decided to buy matching sheets and curtains for my bedroom (yup, even at five, your boy knew how to pull out a color palette!). I remember taking all the birthday money I had saved up—$80!—and asking my mom to take me to Venture (RIP to the old-school Target of the Midwest, one of my go-to places to shop for pretty much anything back then). I walked right up to the blue bedding sets without skipping a beat. As soon as we got home, I ran up to my room, removed the red bedspread and curtains that were there and replaced them with the soothing blues ones (right out of the package! The fabric was still creased and everything). I can remember how excited I was to see the final look as I stepped back to admire my new digs.

The impact was immediate, visceral, undeniable.

In my bones, I knew that the color shift was having a profound effect on my mood and emotional state. To this day, my mom still talks about how I had carefully explained to her that the red made me anxious but the blue made me feel good. I didn't know why, I didn't know how—I just knew it did.

And the rest, as they say, is history.

Now, it wasn't a straight shot to *Queer Eye* from that moment on (not by a country mile!). I've had a circuitous path, to say the least (at one point, I was working the graveyard shift as a gas station attendant while also managing a Bath & Body Works store *and* squeezing in shifts at the Gap). But what I know now—that I didn't know then—was that at five years old, I had just come face-to-face with my life's North Star: my (design) instincts.

And looking back, it's *so* clear that my instincts had been leading me all along.

Believe it or not, I'm 100% self-taught.

Though it took me a minute before I found my way more formally into the world of interior design, my instincts were ever present through all my various gigs, living situations, and seminal moments.

Now, sometimes, my instincts would lead me directly from Point A to Point B. When I was nineteen, I walked into the Great Indoors cold turkey and just point-blank asked for a job, because deep down I knew that I could (a) put together a space and (b) help others to do the same. I got the job on the spot and spent a year there being the #1 salesperson on the floor. (Later, I did the same thing at stores like Bombay Company and Restoration Hardware.)

Other times, I would detour a bit first, and things would have to get worse before they got better. Case in point: My first big apartment complex reno almost got me evicted! True story: I was getting over a breakup and because, for me, home design has always been a massive act of self-care, I proceeded to activate a full-on Bobby Berk Redesign in my unit (i.e., I put in new flooring, painted the kitchen cabinets, and updated the light fixtures). When the super called the building owner in to tattle on me, I genuinely thought I'd be out on the street (again). But instead, the owner took one look at what I had done with the place, turned around, and asked if I could redo the rest of the units in the building. Guess who got free rent for six months because his instincts just refused to be ignored? (Yep, me! The guy who keeps finding that, more than anything, design really is medicine for my mind.)

See? **All good design on some level is always guided by someone's unique and specific instincts.** Home design especially is—because it's *so* personal! It's *your* home so *your* instincts should be calling the shots, not mine! More than any other design project, designing someone's home requires the designer to get to know the homeowner as intimately as possible. I see so much of my job as trying to get into someone's headspace so that I can ultimately make the design choices *they* would make. That way, when the client walks into the finished space, they're saying things like, "Bobby, how did you know?" Or "That's exactly what I would have chosen." The goal isn't just to go in and do a makeover—the goal is to set up the home for *you* and *your* unique needs, passions, loves.

But here's the real reason you need to trust your instincts: When you do, your home automatically becomes **your own personal mental wellness retreat**. And *that's* why I do what I do: Because I've experienced the incredible mental health benefits of a home designed to serve, support, and take care of me and I'm seriously addicted to giving others the same life-changing experience.

I've also noticed that, often, my instincts were the loudest when I was at my lowest. As a lot of you probably already know, it was some of my earliest experiences living *without* a home that impacted—and continues to impact—how I approach home design. When I left my parents' place at fifteen, I was in a tough spot for quite a while before I found my footing. I slept in my car, on friends' couches, and sometimes out on the streets when things were tough. When I was finally able to swing my first apartment—a little one-bedroom apartment on Walnut Street in Springfield, Missouri—I distinctly remember my very first night there like it was yesterday. I had a few hours to myself before my boyfriend at the time got home, and I remember feeling *super* excited to just be left alone to nest a bit. Actually, some friends had invited me to Martha's Vineyard (a local, scene-y nightclub in Springfield, not the bougie island in New England) and even though I wanted to go, I declined because I knew deep down that I needed to take a minute to set up my space. (See? Instincts coming through loud and clear here!)

I set up the kitchen, did some laundry, deep cleaned the bathroom (because of the inconsistent housing situations I've experienced, setting up a new space has always been an important self-care ritual for me). When I finally allowed myself to get under the covers in the first bed behind closed doors I'd slept on in almost two years, it struck me like a quiet bolt of silent lightning.

Even more than physical comfort, I was strangely overcome by a sense of profound peace inside my head—that same, inexplicable, in-my-bones wave of calm I felt when I first saw my blue curtains at five years old. And that's when I realized:

Your home needs to be a safe space for your mind.

Good home design is always good for your mind.

Sometimes, *not* having something is what brings you clarity on what having it really means.

In that moment, I realized that having a secure, stable landing spot at the end of the day is an absolute necessity for your mental wellness. I truly believe that homes are buildings that should not only offer us physical protection but also mental protection. This belief is what continues to drive how I approach home design and, honestly, life. Because **your mental health is the rudder of your entire life** and without it, everything else kind of falls apart.

I knew I was on to something and never stopped holding on to that kernel of wisdom.

It's funny: *Queer Eye*'s slogan is "More Than a Makeover," and I couldn't have said it better myself, honestly. Design is so much more than just giving your home an external makeover—**thoughtfully setting up your home is an act of self-care**, something that is often overlooked. Maybe it's even seen as an extra expense and not a basic necessity.

But the way your home is designed *matters*.

From the floor plan to the color palette all the way down to where you place the sofa and what kind of wall art you choose—all these choices have measurable, tangible effects on your mental state.

Now, with all that being said, will a blue room rid you of your anxiety completely? Probably not. But if your job is a stressful one and a soothing shade of blue in your WFH space gives you even a few moments of calm in the middle of your hectic workday, isn't that more than worth it? Or, conversely, if you struggle with low energy and find that a strategically placed pop of color gives you even a little pick-me-up, why wouldn't you consider it? (And, of course, it goes without saying that you should always seek out the right resources to address your mental health concerns. Design, no matter how thoughtful or intentional, could never replace proper health care for any diagnosis, no matter how big or small.)

My mantra is this: In the end, every little bit counts. I've seen time and time again the IRL tangible results of a space set up to serve, support, and bring genuine joy to the people who use it, and there's no going back for me! The spaces we spend time in are an indispensable part of what our senses (especially our eyes) take in day in and day out. To ignore or disregard the way your spaces are designed is to deprive your mind (and your entire self) of the incredible wellness benefits of a home completely and totally tailored for you and what you need.

So. Now that we know the why, let's get to the how.

How to Read This Book

I can't tell you how thrilled I am that this book is in your hands. I've put together all the hard-won wisdom I've accumulated over my twenty-plus-year career—one that has, more than anything, shown me how to help (re)design people's lives. I hope this book inspires you to, above all else, prioritize your mental health by utilizing the life-changing power of design.

Here's How the Book Breaks Down

In chapter 1, it is all about how important it is to know what makes you happy in life. (Not design. *Life*.) All good design comes from someone's happiness. Because: We've all got instincts! Which means: We can *all* be designers.

In chapter 2, we talk about my #1 mantra: function, function, function. At its core, to design is to improve the *function* of something. It honestly doesn't matter how beautiful something looks—if it doesn't work properly for you/your home/your life, it's gotta go.

In chapter 3, we get down and dirty with cleaning + organization. Will there be tips and inspiring photos? Oh yeah. But more importantly, this chapter will prove once and for all that an organized home is pretty much a mental-wellness love-fest.

Chapter 4 gets into sensory engagement. Design that engages all your senses helps keep you present (which is excellent for your mental health).

In chapter 5, we learn that color is a universal language that speaks to your subconscious (and, therefore, affects your mind). Let's go over all the rules—and then figure out how to break them a little (because you absolutely can).

Chapter 6 highlights *the* most underrated tool for mental wellness: light. Regular sunlight sets everything in motion (sleep cycles, energy levels, even our appetites!). Learn how to harness home design to maximize light so that your space looks—and makes you *feel*—gorgeous.

Chapter 7 is all about plants. Nature is enormously beneficial for our (mental) health, and plants are really the next best thing. Snag some of my go-to styling tips and out-of-the-box (and cost-efficient!) ways to incorporate nature into your home.

I've also put together **guides for every room of the house**—basically, all my best advice for how to customize each room to work as hard as it can for your (mental) health. Fact: Your rooms should work *for* you, not against you!

PRO TIP

You don't have to read this from cover to cover! Feel free to jump around, flip through different sections, or flag pages to come back to. I've also included some workbook activities to help you think through some of my go-to foundational ideas around home design. Think of them as a way to snag a design consult with me via paper + pen!

And one last myth buster for you: Interior designers are generally known as people who are hired to create spaces that cost exorbitant amounts of money. But the truth is, **design is for everyone** and it shouldn't take a fortune to make small changes (often using pieces you already own!) to create a space that supports a calmer state of mind.

I've worked with so many clients over the years, both on and off *Queer Eye*, whose lives have been completely changed by the impact of a home designed to serve them. But you know which client's testimony I continue to find the most powerful?

Mine.

Because that's just it: YOU are your most important client. So let's equip your home to be your best mental wellness advocate, an act that by definition will result in a home that reflects your personal style.

XX,
Bobby

How to Articulate What Makes You Happy

What if I told you that you're really the head designer here, and not me?

It's true! Okay, let me ease you in.

Wherever you are on the "I Know My Style" Spectrum—whether you're 100 percent sure you've been a minimalist since before it was cool or you're 100 percent sure you don't have the first clue what your design style is—taking some time to get reacquainted with yourself and your personal preferences is never a bad idea. Your style may have changed since the last time you've set up your space (this is totally normal and okay!), in which case this chapter will probably feel more like a quick software update (but one you won't want to hit snooze on). Or maybe the way your space needs to function has changed as a result of a natural life transition or a shift in priorities, making this chapter a much-needed reset for you. Whatever the case may be, it's important to have a general sense of your current style before starting any design project to make the most of your time, resources, and energy.

Don't know what your current design style is? Well, here's the good news: **Your design style is literally Anything That Makes You Happy.** And coincidentally—or not so coincidentally—things that make you happy are simply, profoundly (and scientifically) awesome for your mental health. So there you have it: Knowing your design style *is* a mental health necessity, through and through. (And it's okay if what makes you happy doesn't formally have a name like midcentury modern or boho chic. We'll get to all that, trust me!)

Our first order of business, then, is to figure out how to actually *articulate* what makes you happy because, for lots of people, that's not easy (especially when it comes to home design). But what I'm gonna show you in this chapter is that people who claim "not to know their design style" actually do. That's because your design style comes from, well, *you*—your unique likes and dislikes, preferences, and favorite things in *all* aspects of your life, not just design. It's not about what kind of furniture you'd pick out—it's about what car you'd drive, what your last meal would be, what you'd binge-watch on a rainy day, where your dream vacation would be.

Using these organic data points as your starting place is a foolproof way to get to the ultimate Home Design Finish Line: **a home that not only "feels like you" but, by virtue of reflecting what you love, is also a serotonin-boosting, happiness-producing space that's hyper-customized to improve your mental wellness.** Because it's not a stretch to say that mental wellness is quite literally everything. Without your "control center" intact, the quality of the rest of your life just won't be what you need and deserve.

So let's get to it! Learning how to **honor what makes you happy** strengthens your home design muscle. It's time to get your reps in.

ABOVE: Book lovers, rejoice: Any curation of your favorite hardcovers can inspire a color palette or visual display. Bonus: These sculptural objects also double as bookends (I love a good multitasker).

OPPOSITE: Personalize any room by making your favorite graphic print the focal point. Serene, earth tones add contrast without competing.

So. What Makes You "Happy"?

Let's break it down.

Okay, let's be real. "What makes you happy?" is kind of a loaded question. Or, at the very least, a not-so-straightforward question. You may be thinking, "In what context?" or "In what area of my life?" or "It really depends on the situation."

It's a concept that has stumped lots of people across the board throughout millennia and has probably been thought about, written about, argued about, and podcasted to death. And while I'm definitely not here to give you a philosophy lecture, what I am going to help you do is **unpack how to *think* about happiness, both in general and as it relates to home design.** There are so many ways to make a happy choice in life and none of them are "more correct" than any of the others. The first thing to consider is that there are other words that can mean *happy* or represent a genuine sense of happiness. So if the word *happy* feels too difficult to pin down, try using some of my go-tos:

calm	**joyful**
safe	**purposeful**
inspired	**peaceful**
fun	**energized**

At this stage, you don't even really have to know why you like something. (Though, if you do, that's great! Definitely use that to help you make some design decisions while not letting it limit you too much, either.) Often, a theme or style will reveal itself pretty organically after you notice a pattern or realize that you've been selecting certain types of items, prints, or colors. But, for right now, the rule of thumb is this: **If you're drawn to it, it counts.**

Your instincts are the CEO of this project. (And don't worry: There are ways of incorporating all the seemingly different things that make you happy into a cohesive design plan for a space. That's where I come in—I got you every step of the way.) But we're not there yet. Right now, we're just focusing on learning to **trust your own instincts,** something every good designer (and every mentally healthy human!) has to learn how to do.

It's okay to love what you love.

Trendless Advice

What makes you happy may or may not coincide with the latest design trends and, TBH, that doesn't really matter at the end of the day. As my friend Tan France put it once, "I don't give a s*** about fashion. What I care about is style." I couldn't agree more—trends will come and go and it's always fun to switch things up when budget and resources permit, but true personal style will always be timeless.

23

Happiness Is a Muscle

Your *only* job here is to clock when you feel excited. What do you feel drawn to? (Don't overthink it!) Remember: We can totally build an entire look off a single detail (or several details). And yes, design should be *this* much fun!

Let's warm it up.

YOU: I like some of this but not all of this.

ME: Great! Let's go with *just* the part you like.

YOU: Oooh!

ME: I know, right?!

HOW TO ARTICULATE WHAT MAKES YOU HAPPY

The
Home Design
Golden Rule:
If you love it,
it will work.

The Happiness
Gut Check(list)

→ SOMETHING THAT REMINDS YOU OF
someone you love

→ SOMETHING THAT REMINDS YOU OF
the last time you felt safe

→ SOMETHING THAT **motivates
or energizes you**

→ SOMETHING THAT **engages your senses**

→ SOMETHING THAT **elicits strong,
positive emotion**

→ SOMETHING THAT **smells awesome**

→ SOMETHING THAT MAKES YOU FEEL
comforted or cozy

→ SOMETHING THAT MAKES YOU FEEL
supported or taken care of

→ SOMETHING THAT **takes stuff
off your plate**

→ SOMETHING THAT **anticipates your needs**

→ SOMETHING THAT MAKES YOU FEEL LIKE YOU'RE
moving toward a goal

HOW TO ARTICULATE WHAT MAKES YOU HAPPY

Q: ~~What's your design~~ aesthetic?

A: Let's
normalize
NOT asking
this question
Ever.

It should be clear by now that this question isn't really where I recommend starting. I've found over the years that it's just too broad to be helpful, especially if you've never really thought about it before. Trying to answer it is honestly intimidating and will probably catapult your mind into a hectic scramble to try to remember the last thing you saw on Pinterest, google a BuzzFeed quiz, or recall something vaguely interesting you saw in the rogue *Architectural Digest* you were riffling through while waiting for your last teeth cleaning.

Because here's the thing: If I have you look through a bunch of interior design photos and ask you to pick one, you'll invariably start making a list of all the things you have to buy to replicate exactly what you see. And while that might make for a great IG post or compliments the next time you have people over (all great things, btw!), I don't think it's the best way to create a space that reflects your *true* style, nor would it maximize your mental wellness because it wouldn't be personalized to you.

Besides, the best designs often defy labels anyway. (At least mine do!) Good design can certainly have a loose direction and foundational ideas but, in the end, will usually end up being a unique, interesting, and harmonious mix of different styles.

So I say we change the conversation. Ready?

Let's find a jumping-off point you're excited about—and build from there.

Remember, a jumping-off point could be literally anything. A color, a shape, a smell even. A photograph, a hobby, a song. (Don't worry, I've got lots of starting points for you if you're beginning to feel lost again! The rest of this chapter is pretty much Starting Point City.)

The Closeted Truth

Home is where the answers are.

What's probably becoming clear by now is that when it comes to personal style, you've been sitting on the answers to the test. (Feel that surge of self-confidence? Say hello to your instincts. They've been there the whole time—trust me!)

Still don't believe me? Let's take a look in your closet, shall we? I often get a lot of my ideas for texture, color palettes, and general style from a quick peek at someone's fashion choices. (And, no, I didn't get this idea from Tan—I've actually been utilizing this trick for years!) Whether or not you think of yourself as a "fashion-conscious" person, the choices you make with your clothing—even if you think they're mindless or purely practical—are still, on some level, conscious decisions you're making to express yourself out in the world. And that means **you *do* have a style**—it's just a matter of having your friendly neighborhood designer point it out to ya.

Over the years, I've come to find that the closet comes the closest to someone's home design style because of how personal clothing choices are, but, really, you can do this with any area of your life. Try scoping out your kitchen, the way you've arranged your workspace, or seeing what's on your nightstand or vanity. Almost treat this exercise as if you'd broken into your own home and are looking for "clues" about yourself, which is, incidentally, what I do on *Queer Eye* a lot of the time! When we first barge in on our heroes, I always glean as much information as I can from the way a home is initially set up to make sure the new design really reflects who our hero is as opposed to designing a shiny new home that doesn't actually feel representative of the homeowner's true self.

Ooh, shoe-lover alert. It's giving me Carrie Bradshaw vibes circa the first three seasons—based on this, I'd go for a neutral palette with pops of color.

CHUNKY SWEATERS ——————————→

CHUNKY THROW

LEATHER JACKET ——————————→

LEATHER SOFA

PLAID SHIRTS ——————————→

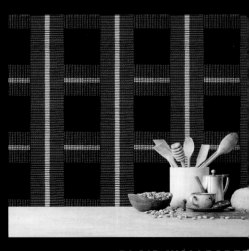

PLAID WALLPAPER

Found in Translation

Inspiration can come from anywhere.

When I say anything that makes you happy can be translated into a design style, I mean *anything*. Check out some of my favorite style inspirations that resulted in some amazing pieces, accents, and spaces.

Even your favorite fruit can be inspiration! This durian lover opted for a cool, nubby accent pillow that, yes, reminds him of his favorite fruit. (Hey, you love what you love. I'm here for it.)

This music lover had a massive collection of albums—including a set of duplicates— so I turned some of them into wall art (zero-waste design for the win).

The best
way to
predict
your future
is to create it.

- Abraham Lincoln

ABOVE: I love anchoring a gallery wall with a favorite mantra, quote, or saying— it makes any room feel super personal right away.

OPPOSITE: Boho-inspired color palettes don't usually incorporate deep blue hues, but if you love it, it will work. Every damn time.

Design for Where You Want to Go

Good design should put gas in your tank.

Studies show that you're happiest when you feel you're making progress toward a goal. This may seem intuitive . . . or does it? Often, people think that reaching the actual mountaintop will make you happier. ("If I could just land that promotion, I'll be happier." "If I could become a homeowner, I'll be happier." "If I find a partner, I'll be happier.") But as many studies will attest, human beings are actually not that good at predicting what makes them happy. "Happiness . . . is a fast-moving target. As passionate as we are about finding it, we routinely misforecast what will make us happy, how long our joy will last, and how intense it will be." (Marianna Pogosyan, PhD, *Psychology Today*)

And let's be honest: We didn't need a study to come along and tell us that, right? There are tons of people in the world who have everything they could possibly want and are clearly miserable. Conversely, there are people who have next to nothing and are incredibly joyful.

So, since what *has* proven to enhance your well-being is the chase—and meeting smaller milestones along the way intensifies this dopamine hit, by the way—then that means forward momentum is the goal. Professor of psychology Timothy A. Pychyl notes in *Psychology Today* that "to the extent that we're making progress on our goals, we're happier emotionally and more satisfied with our lives."

Now here's where I come in: **Home design is an *incredibly powerful way* to help you achieve your goals.**

As a designer, I've seen this in action countless times, both during *Queer Eye* and with my clients outside the show. Witnessing the profound impact of creating a space tailored to helping people meet their goals never gets old for me. It's truly one of the deepest joys I get to experience as a designer. The effect goal-oriented design has on someone's mental wellness is so palpable, so indisputable, and so, *so* real. What I've realized—and witnessed firsthand time and time again—is that good design has the power to literally remove blockages in your life. When you clear a path for a way forward by creating a space that encourages, elicits, and promotes action toward a meaningful life goal, your mental health improves dramatically.

Good design has the power to literally remove blockages in your life.

HOW TO ARTICULATE WHAT MAKES YOU HAPPY

A Note on Grief

Your home is often the first place where grief becomes apparent—though, by nature, this is easier to spot from the outside looking in. That's because common symptoms of the grieving process—general neglect, accumulation of someone's old belongings, and an inability to maintain basic cleanliness and organization—are born, develop, and live subconsciously. More often than not, it takes someone outside the grieving individual to come in with fresh eyes and gently bring to light what's happening and how mired in grief he/she/they have been (something we see happen on *Queer Eye* all the time—in fact, this is often the Fab Five's first order of business). For grief and so many other mental states, your home—unbeknownst to you—becomes a mirror image of your inner life.

When it comes to someone dealing with the loss of a loved one (or any other life event where a period of grieving is necessary), it's so important to acknowledge first and foremost that grief is an individual process. It's not a one-size-fits-all phenomenon by any measure.

As a designer, I've learned that I'm in a unique and privileged position to help walk people through phases of their grieving process as I work through a redesign with them. And the tough truth that I often help my clients confront is that staying inside grief that's now manifesting as dysfunction, disrepair, and disarray is not only unhealthy but, by the client's full and honest admission, also not actually commemorating the wishes of their deceased loved one. From a home design standpoint, it's often facing the reality that your grief is physically preventing your home from functioning optimally for your current life and future goals. Working through future design plans in a space that's stuck in a place of grief is always a delicate negotiation—I have to find the middle ground between honoring someone's memory and giving clients that gentle nudge toward moving on. And as tough as it is, one of the most rewarding aspects of my job is showing people that design can provide practical tools to help you heal and move forward.

While this absolutely requires a case-by-case approach, more often than not I've found that simply coming alongside someone in grief to acknowledge their pain is incredibly powerful. Once I've built enough trust, one of the first things I coach clients through is making the decision to start clearing out space in the home (a task that's clearly just as much mental wellness–related as it is design-related). And while I always approach someone grieving with the utmost sensitivity, respect, and love, I do also have a rule of thumb when it comes to working through a space that has clearly been taken over and made dysfunctional by someone's grief.

If something is helping you heal, you'll notice that while you may feel pangs of sadness and nostalgia when you interact with it (whether it's a small knickknack, a keepsake, or a photo), those feelings don't overtake you to the point where you can't move forward. If seeing or interacting with an item rips the wound back open (often because of the way it currently lives in your home, i.e., it's constantly in your line of sight or multiple items are clustered throughout the home, making the entire space one massive emotional landmine), it's a sign that the current design is actively keeping you from moving forward in a healthy way.

Something as simple as dedicating a contained space—be it a gallery wall, a shelf, or even just a single spot on your bookcase—is a great way to commemorate a loved one while still keeping the majority of the space in your home optimized for your future goals. Often, getting yourself to even take this kind of step may feel incredibly hard. But I promise that once you do, you'll have taken that first baby step forward toward a healing process that keeps you moving and, most important, living your life to the fullest—which, by all measures, is the best way to honor your loved ones.

Need a Design Consult?

Right this way.

Home design is like anything else that's reflective of your personality—it tends to be an organic mix of a bunch of different aspects of your life. I can't tell you how many clients I've worked with who at first claim to know nothing about their design style but, after I start asking the right questions, realize very quickly that . . . they do! In a matter of minutes, their design style reveals itself with crystal clarity. And guess how many of my questions were "design" questions? Zero.

That's because happiness IRL (the #1 place your design style should come from) stems from so many different parts of your life. I've found that the best way to approach figuring out your style, especially if you genuinely feel you have no idea what your style is, is to (1) take the pressure off, (2) pour yourself a drink, and (3) just think about all the other things in your life you like/love/are obsessed with. Your favorite meal, your tendency to wear sneakers over boots, that movie you can watch over and over again without ever getting sick of it. **Don't get hung up on the fact that you don't know how to "pick" a design style—just think about all the other things in your life that make you damn happy.** I promise you'll not only find yourself fully immersed in a "style" but also realize, like Dorothy, that you had the power to bring yourself home all along.

FILL-IN-THE-BLANK *happy*

I'VE ALWAYS WANTED TO TAKE A TRIP TO _____.

I LOVE THE WAY _____ DRESSES.

IF I COULD EAT ANYTHING FOR THE REST OF MY LIFE, IT WOULD BE _____

_____.

MY ALL-TIME FAVORITE TV SHOW IS _____.

IF I HAD A DAY OFF OF WORK, HERE'S HOW I'D SPEND THE DAY: _____

_____

_____.

IF YOU LOOKED IN MY CLOSET, YOU'D SEE A LOT OF _____

_____.

WHEN I'M HAVING A BAD DAY, I LIKE TO _____

_____.

THE SPOTIFY PLAYLISTS I HAVE ON REPEAT ARE _____.

IF MONEY WAS NOT AN ISSUE, I WOULD BE A _____.

WHENEVER _____ IS HAVING A SALE, I'M 100 PERCENT
UNREACHABLE. (DON'T EVEN TRY.)

A LOT OF PEOPLE DON'T KNOW THAT I'M SECRETLY A BIG FAN OF _____

_____.

BEFORE I DIE, I WANT TO SEE _____ IN CONCERT.

#NOFILTER

I try not to edit myself too much, even at the moodboard stage. Making an unexpected connection, seeing a fun color palette materialize, or coming up with something totally out of the box—all of these things are born from a kind of free-association, there-are-no-bad-ideas type of thinking. So your moodboard should reflect that.

Ready. Set. Moodboard.

(aka the fun part)

Now that we've unearthed the right information about what makes you happy, it's time to go into full designer mode: Moodboards, here we come. This is one of my favorite steps during a design process because it allows me to see all of a client's interests, preferences + personality attributes in one visual mash-up. You can definitely add in design elements and photos of spaces you like and are inspired by, but don't feel compelled to (in fact, it's actually more fun if you don't at this stage!). A good moodboard helps you connect the dots, pull out visual themes and patterns, and, most important, stay inspired—basically, it's where the magic happens!

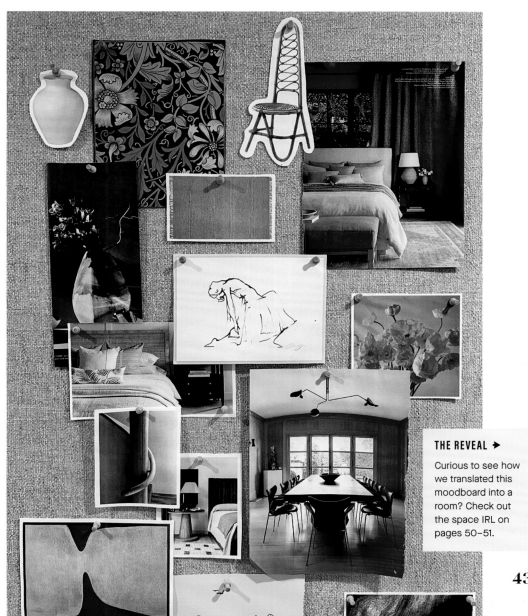

THE REVEAL ➤

Curious to see how we translated this moodboard into a room? Check out the space IRL on pages 50–51.

MY MOODBOARD

Colors that put me in a damn good mood

Words I say a lot

A cool texture/ pattern/print I keep coming back to

YUM

**Don't know why,
but I DIG these**

Style icons

Wish I was here

Designing with Intention

Design around what you love and for the life you want.

What I hope is clear by this point is that being super intentional about the design choices you make for your home has a measurable effect on your mental wellness. Whether it's taking your happiness a little more seriously or tackling a deeper clean-out somewhere in your home, design inherently goes far beyond just decorating. It's a profound act of self-care, the effects of which you'll notice both instantly and over time.

What I also want to make clear is that home design isn't necessarily a call to spend or invest massive amounts of money (though if you're able to budget for larger-scale projects, that's fantastic!). So much of what I cover in this book requires little to no money because, like happiness, good design doesn't come from making huge purchases (though, yes, it can cost money at times!). The ultimate litmus test for good design is whether or not it works for and serves *you*.

Now, more than ever, our homes are being asked to work even harder and function in more ways (and for longer stretches of time). Alongside the many other ways we try to be kind to our minds, I believe (and know for a fact because I've witnessed it countless times) that planning out the place where you spend the most time—with thoughtfulness and deep consideration for your preferences, needs, and goals—will yield a real, tangible return on your investment. And investing in your mental wellness—the one thing that literally affects every other part of your life—is undoubtedly the best decision you'll ever make.

The ultimate litmus test for good design is whether or not it works for and serves you.

OPPOSITE: Love switching up your accessories from time to time? An L-shaped couch in a neutral shade is the perfect blank canvas for you to go nuts.

ABOVE: Not afraid of commitment? A sofa in a bold and unexpected shade—like this moody mustard—is an easy, one-and-done way to personalize a living room. Want to see how the full space turned out? Jump to page 58.

49

Chapter 1
The Good Bits

What makes you happy is pretty much the most important thing ever (score).

Your happiness is the penultimate twofer: It's the foundation for both good home design and great mental health.

We're retiring the question "What's your design style?" (You're welcome.) Instead, find a **jumping-off point** (aka *anything*—a sofa, a chair, or a weirdly shaped vase you saw on someone's IG) that gets you excited and take it from there.

THE NEW
Living Room
Manifesto

THE ULTIMATE GUIDE TO A HEALTHY, HAPPY LIVING SPACE

We believe THAT LIVING ROOMS ARE THE NEW PINCH HITTERS.

We believe IN THE POWER OF PLANNING OUT YOUR SPACE.

We believe THAT LIVING ROOMS SHOULD BE ABOUT CONNECTION.

We believe THAT YOU SHOULD BE PARTY-READY AT ALL TIMES.

We believe THAT ANYTHING CAN BE A SOFA (LITERALLY ANYTHING).

We believe THAT LIVING ROOMS ARE THE NEW PINCH HITTERS.

Living rooms are now full-on casual (and I for one am here for it!). Gone are the stiff remnants of for-company-only parlors. The modern living room is now a space used for, well, *living* (aka taking conference calls, eating full-on meals, napping, chilling, playing, and, of course, sitting with abandon for looooong periods of time). Needing to multitask and be highly functional all while still being easy on the eyes is a pretty tall order, so it's important to prioritize pieces, details, and colors you won't get tired of, ones that do double (and triple) duty and, most important, that make you really happy.

Meet the living room that doubles as a podcast studio that also moonlights as a reading nook, thanks to the super cozy throw and air-cleaning plants in the corner. (What a show-off.)

We believe IN THE POWER OF PLANNING OUT YOUR SPACE.

Mastering the Art of Furniture Arranging

Arranging a space is never really a done deal, but that's kind of the beauty of it. Life is full of transitions, and it's important to meet yourself where you're at and design your space to do the exact same thing. Aside from some across-the-board don'ts, there's really nothing you can't do. As long as you start with function (what do you actually need your living room to do?), you're gold.

Go with the (Feng Shui) Flow

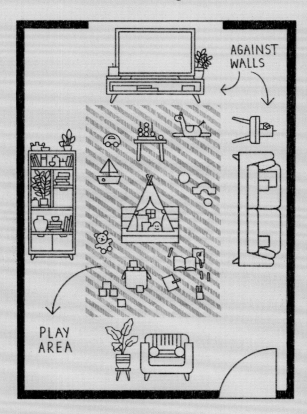

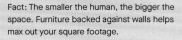

Fact: The smaller the human, the bigger the space. Furniture backed against walls helps max out your square footage.

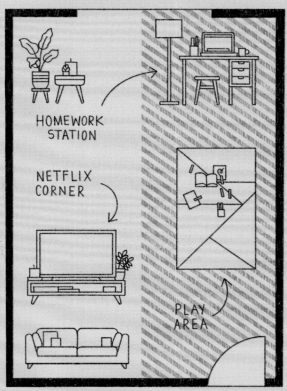

Let's go Dutch: Homework station right, Netflix corner left. Mind the gap.

We believe THAT ALL LIVING ROOMS SHOULD BE ABOUT CONNECTION.

Happy Moments Everywhere You Look

Your living room should be a space that makes it easy to *connect*—whether that's with others or with yourself after a long day. Think of this room as your personal welcome home sign, your "hey you made it" hug, your reset. Especially if it's your first pit stop upon entering, be sure to incorporate details that make you feel instantly happy on sight.

Fun, patterned pillows make any corner an instant curl-up-and-get-cozy spot (and you can never have too many of those).

Coffee-table books should be easy on the eyes and easy to reach for. Curate your favorites so they're ready to grab when you're in the mood for a leisurely read.

Carve out a spot for your morning ritual with a resting spot for your paper and cup of joe (that also doubles as extra guest seating).

A device-less room doesn't have to be boring. Replace the "TV spot" with an interesting visual display.

We believe THAT YOU SHOULD BE PARTY-READY AT ALL TIMES.

Hosting Is Really About Community

A huge part of keeping your mental health in tip-top shape is regular connection with loved ones. So when your home isn't guest-ready on a very basic level, it's just way too easy to stay isolated. While having alone time is definitely a part of living a balanced life (and for introverts, a very necessary state of being), it's also important to incorporate regular time with others—and design a living room that's conducive to gathering—to maintain your mental health. In other words: Stay ready so you don't have to get ready. Give your living room the quick, can-I-have-someone-over gut check (can you seat one to two more people, do you have a few extra glasses, can you do a speedy five-minute tidy sesh?).

We believe THAT ANYTHING CAN BE A SOFA (LITERALLY ANYTHING).

The Ultimate Unexpected Seating Guide

Here's my gentle nudge for ya: There's no excuses! You *can* have people over—here are some of my favorite, non-sofa sofas for spaces that need some extra-creative seating solutions.

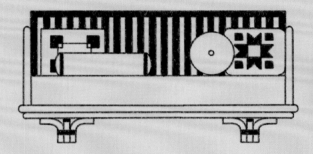

THE CASE FOR THE DAYBED

TBH, it's really a couch that moonlights as a bed. Either way, it's the twofer every small space needs.

THE OTTOMAN: IT CAN SERIOUSLY DO EVERYTHING

The footrest-turned-extra-seat-turned-coffee-table (aka the ultimate multi-hyphenate).

THE FLOOR PLAN

Here's the plan: Throw massive cushions all over the floor. Done and done.

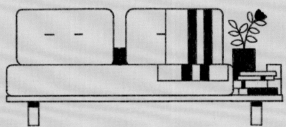

DON'T BENCH YOUR CUSHIONS

Add a few throw pillows and your favorite blanket and voilà—hello, cute seating area.

Bobby-pedia

An incomplete but still super useful work-in-progress list of terms, phrases + expressions I use in design/life

A ———

ACCENT: A detail, object, area— or *moment*, in *QE*-speak—that acts as a visual exclamation point; often stands out in sharp contrast with its surroundings; i.e., an accent wall

B ———

BALANCE: The distribution of visual weight (yes, this is a thing! See *Visual Weight*) when doing pretty much anything in the design world (styling objects, choosing colors, integrating textures)

BOBBERZ: JVN's favorite thing to yell out when he can't stand how much he loves my makeovers

C ———

CHAOS: The state of utter mayhem, mess + mind-blowing disorder in any given space that's both physically and mentally harmful

CONTRAST: The effect of creating visual difference, whether it's through color, shape, finish, or texture (and, personally, one of my all-time favorite effects to implement when I want to quickly juhj up a space)

D ———

DEPTH: The dimension and visual distance you see from viewing a three-dimensional object or space; often referred to as an "illusion" designers create to make small spaces look bigger/wider/deeper

E ———

ECLECTIC: A cool AF look that combines ideas and elements from a diverse range of styles

ELEVATE: To clean up or polish; to make more refined (see *Juhj*)

F ———

FENG SHUI: literally translated as "the way of wind and water." The ancient Chinese art of arranging buildings, objects, and space to achieve harmony with the elements of the natural world (aka my go-to guide for maximizing the flow of positive energy in any space I design)

FOCAL POINT: An area, element, or item with the most visual weight or dominance; what attracts the eye first in a space

G ———

GAY FAIRY GODMOTHER: An alter ego persona I (and my Fab Five besties) tap into when we use our respective talents to make amazing s*** happen

GAY HELL: Any thing, situation, or state of affairs that would cause a reasonable gay human to freak TF out

It's your life. Design it well.

H

HOME DESIGN: The way a home is personalized and planned out to support the mental wellness, unique personality, and life goals of its occupant(s)

HOT MESS: The proper way to describe something or someone that has basically gone to s***

I

INTEREST: Literally something—anything!—that's interesting (aka NOT boring) to the eye/senses (Note: You can microdose this with smaller items or go all out—paint a wall or invest in a conversation-starting couch)

IT'S YOUR LIFE. DESIGN IT WELL: My mantra, M.O., and message to the world (if I could write anything on a billboard, it would probably be this)

J

JTIO (JUST THROW IT OUT): The thing you must say—loudly + proudly—in response to anything you find in your home that (1) you've honestly grown out of, (2) will cost more to fix than replace, or (3) will not, in its current state, prove useful or functional to you/ your life

JUHJ: To snatch [*insert double fingersnaps here*]; to spiff up or take up a notch (see *Elevate*)

K

KNOWLEDGE OF YOUR SINGULAR, AWESOME, ONE-OF-A-KIND SELF: All of the many interesting, cool, and fun things that you like, you love, reflect your personality, and define the unique human being that you are (this will, among other things, inform your home design style)

L

LINE OF SIGHT: The visible range or area in your eyesight's direct path (what falls in this area gets a straight shot to your brain + nervous system so be very mindful of this at any given spot in your home)

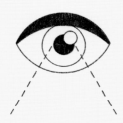

M

MENTAL WELLNESS: An optimal state of well-being that allows you to cope with the normal stresses of life, be productive, and make a contribution to the world

N

NONFUNCTIONAL: Used to describe anything that doesn't work optimally to support you, your current goals, and/or the way you want to live your life

NOOK: A small, recessed spot or corner, often found in a kitchen (breakfast nooks are my fave!

O

ORGANIC: Uncontrived; intentionally irregular; resembling or suggesting forms found in nature IRL

ORGANIZATION: A set of systems, rules, and order put in place to keep your s*** together (an absolute nonnegotiable when it comes to setting up your home to support your mental health!)

P

PATINA: The character-packed, timeworn luster or finish on any surface that comes from natural wear + tear and/or polishing (I love a good patina, especially on a leather sofa or a solid wood table)

PRIDE: The all-day, everyday state of mind and social movement dedicated to the self-affirming dignity, equality, and increased visibility of the LGBTQIA+ community.

Q

QUEER EYE-APPROVED: Used to describe anything—design, article of clothing, a life choice—that the Fab Five would unanimously sign off on (e.g., taking time for yourself? 100 percent *Queer Eye*-approved)

R

RESET: The fresh start we all need sometimes when we're experiencing a big life transition, seasonal shift, or change in circumstances and/or priorities (the need for a reset often signals a need for a redesign in the home, too)

THE REVEAL: The gorgeous "after" that follows the tragic "before," or the "Let's-skip-to-the-good-part" moment in all its glory when I show you the Bobbified magic of a space I've reimagined to look, feel, and function better for its user(s)

S

SCALE: Proportion; the way an object's size in a space relates to the sizes of other objects in the same space

SELF-CARE: Anything (and I mean *anything*) you do that supports your physical, mental, and emotional health and contributes to your overall happiness and general well-being

STYLE: An external, physical, and visible expression of whatever makes you happy

T

TEXTILES: Cloth or goods produced by weaving, knitting, or felting (aka the slightly more insider-y term for basically any type of fabric)

TEXTURE: The visual and/or tactile quality of a surface (and my preferred way of adding contrast and interest to a space)

U

UNFINISHED PROJECT: The dust-collecting, guilt-inducing result of procrastination that often comes from lack of proper support, resources, and/or an emotional block you may be avoiding

V

VISUAL WEIGHT: A designer-y term used to measure or indicate how much something attracts the eye (i.e., the more an element attracts the eye, the greater its visual weight)

W

WELLNESS-INSPIRED DESIGN: Design and/or architecture focused on the well-being of its users; use of materials and color palettes inspired by nature; elements of biophilic design (connecting architecture and nature) and outdoor-indoor space integration

X

XX: My go-to way to sign off, and out (and how I greet the people I love IRL)

Y

YAS, QWEEN: A Fab Five–ism commonly used in moments of great excitement for a particularly beautiful, encouraging, and/or milestone-y moment in a hero's journey; also appropriate when expressing pretty much any positive emotion (e.g., Work meeting canceled? Yas, Qween!)

Z

ZADDY VIBES: Energy that is confident and snatched AF (e.g., if you're happy and feeling yourself, you're giving major zaddy vibes)

ACCENT

CONTRAST

INTEREST

BALANCE

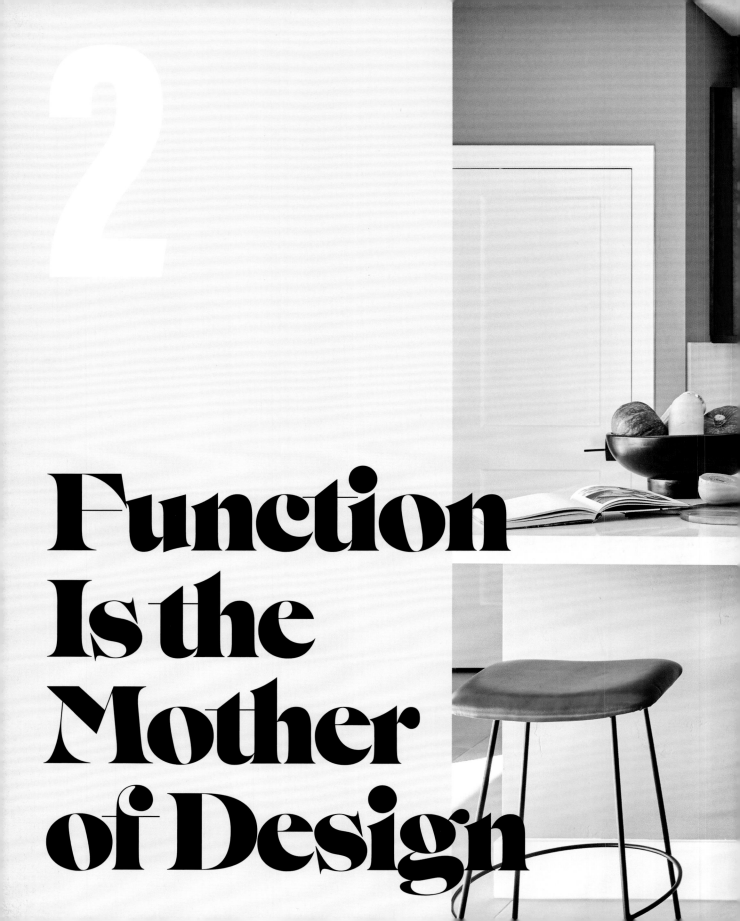

2

Function Is the Mother of Design

Let's talk about how your home is designed.

And I don't just mean what it looks like (though, yes, that's definitely part of it). I'm talking about the whole package—it's not just the color of your sofa; it's the location of your sofa. It's not just how your bed looks; it's also how your bed feels. It's not just how a room is "supposed" to be used; it's the five other things you do in this room that you probably didn't design around (Zoom conference corner in the kids' playroom, I'm looking at you). The sum total of the million and a half big decisions, micro decisions, and all the in-between-size decisions you've made in order to set up your home is what I mean when I refer to how your home is designed.

Because here's the big secret: Home design at its core really refers to **how your home works.** Top to bottom, end to end, start to finish—if your home doesn't work, aka **function**, the way it needs to for you not just to live your life but also to maximize your quality of life, it's a design fail, through and through (no matter how pretty it looks). And design fails in the home wreak utter havoc on your mental health. Which brings us to the million-dollar question we'll unpack in this next chapter: **Is your current (home) design working for you?**

At its core, home design is really about how your home works.

Design Is the Pre-game

Before we jump in, a few preliminary notes: This isn't going to be a list of what to buy and where to shop (though I've got tons of recs if you're at a place where you're ready to invest in some new pieces!). Design—and life, coincidentally—is so much more than buying things. (It *is* about buying the *right* things, though. But we'll get to that in a sec.) The heart of what design is starts eons before the "big reveal": It's all the prep, forethought, and consideration you put into equipping your space for *how it's going to be used IRL*. Or, here's the one-word definition:

Designing is planning.

It's the thing you think through *before* you pull out the credit card, the dress rehearsal where you work out the kinks *before* the big show.

THE PLAN IS THE THING

Great design can result only from a great design **plan.** You wouldn't start a meal without a recipe to guide your meal prep. Or embark on an amazing road trip without figuring out your itinerary first.

"Let's eat beef bourguignon!" → 1 2 3 4 5 → **THE FINISHED MEAL**

"Let's go on a road trip!" 1 2 3 4 5 → **THE FINAL DESTINATION**

"Let's update the living room!" 1 2 3 4 5 → **THE GORGEOUS, FINAL DESIGN**

This is where the magic happens!

Design Is Also the Post-game

Design also happens *after* you think you're done designing. (Because when your needs change, your design should, too.) I get calls and texts from *QE* heroes all the time asking about tips on where to move couches, or how to rearrange the kids' rooms as they get older, etc., because often the *re*design is where you can really get things right—after you've gathered more IRL data around what's been working or not working or what needs to be tweaked after a few hiccups. Chairs starting to wobble? Let's invest here. Need more storage? Let's free up the wall. Kids getting taller? Let's phase pieces out.

Hmm, something's missing.

Hello, color, depth, and tons of personality!

While at first avoiding color in tighter rooms might seem like the way to go, doing so means you risk a space looking too flat or sterile. Strategically placed colors and shapes actually bring depth to a smaller space (not to mention tons of personality).

Design is never a one-and-done; it's always an ongoing process.

FUN(CTIONAL)
Mad Libs

Here's some homework to get your home to work (see what I did there?). Before tackling any space, it's important to honestly assess what's working and what's not from a function standpoint.

IF I COULD WAVE A MAGIC DESIGN WAND, THIS SPACE WOULD SUPPORT ME/SERVE MY WELLNESS BY HELPING ME _____

_____.

WHEN I'M IN THIS ROOM, I WANT TO FEEL _____.

I THINK WHAT'S CURRENTLY WORKING WELL IN THIS SPACE IS _____

_____.

MY FAVORITE THING TO DO IN THIS ROOM RIGHT NOW IS _____.

WHAT I WISH WORKED BETTER IN THIS ROOM IS _____

_____.

THE THING THAT MOST ANNOYS ME ABOUT THIS ROOM IS _____.

_____ WORKS DECENTLY BUT IS KIND OF AN EYESORE.

_____ IS A PIECE I LOVE BUT, TBH, IT FAILS TO _____.

I'D REALLY LOVE FOR THIS ROOM TO HELP ME ACHIEVE _____.
                                                    [SPECIFIC GOAL]

I WISH _____

HAPPENED MORE FREQUENTLY/REGULARLY IN THIS ROOM.

HERE'S A LIST OF ALL ACTIVITIES THAT REGULARLY HAPPEN IN THIS SPACE: _____

_____

_____.

It's still important to point out what *is* working so we can identify reasons why certain activities happen and why others don't. Love lounging in your bedroom because of the awesome, cushy blankets and soothing color palette? Well, that's also prob why you can't get any work done in there, which might mean you should try to set up your WFH space elsewhere OR carve out a space where you're mindful of what's in your line of sight (i.e., DON'T face your bed. It's too tempting).

How will you live in this room?

When you think through what you need a room to do—both practically and emotionally—at the start of the design process, you're guaranteeing the maximum return on investment in terms of how it'll make you feel at the end.

Function always leads my entire exploration process at the beginning of any project. Form is what follows once I know exactly how a space needs to work for its users.

Yes, there are some aspects of design that are purely decorative. (Food for thought: Adding visual interest to a space actually is kind of a function in and of itself IMO because beauty serves a purpose.) But without function driving the design plan, you're really just putting together a museum exhibit or, at best, a fake "model home" as opposed to a home that functions IRL, for real life, for real people. Ultimately, form and function are inseparable, but function should always be the first filter.

➤ FULL-FRONTAL STORAGE

Sink consoles with open shelving makes things like extra linens easily visible for your guests (so they don't have to initiate an all-drawer search party for extra TP).

THE WORK/PLAY-FROM-HOME ROOM

Homework station? Check.
Zoom meeting spot? Check.
A place for a quick Zoom
meeting *while* watching
someone do homework? Check.
(See, multitasking is easy.)

Floating shelves to the rescue.
Transform any awkward, unused
corner into a highly functional
storage spot.

FORM + FUNCT

[fawrm]

noun

1. external **appearance**; configuration

2. the **shape** of a thing or person

The way it looks

[fuhngk-shuhn]

noun

1. the **purpose** for which something is designed or exists; role.

verb; used without object

2. to have or exercise a function; **serve**

what it does for you

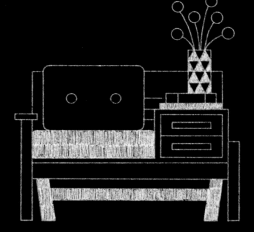

ION = DESIGN

[d(ə)-zīn]

verb; used with object

1. to prepare the preliminary sketch or the **plans** for (a work to be executed), especially to plan the form and structure of

2. to **plan** and fashion the form and structure of an object, work of art, decorative scheme, etc.

The final space that's been planned out for a specific purpose (and looks beautiful _AF_)

Maximize Your Work-Arounds

Whatever you can't change, you're kinda choosing (for now).

Whether you're in a rental or just not in the market for big renovations at the moment, there are lots of reasons you'd need to work around your current space. I get it! But many of the *ways* you've chosen to work around things you can't control (an awkward floor plan, countertops you aren't going to upgrade just yet, rental appliances) are all still functional design decisions. Did you *choose* to store your chopping knives in the drawer farthest from your cutting boards? (If you did, Antoni and I are both rolling our eyes lovingly.) Well, that's a design decision! Are your favorite sneakers hidden under a pile of boxes of who-knows-what in the garage? Also a design decision—and a fashion one. (We get down and dirty with organization in chapter 3, but if you want to get a head start, jump to page 102.) Or maybe you decided to forgo landscaping in favor of another purchase for your home, but your family is an outdoorsy bunch. Well, that's gonna affect everyone's wellness (including yours when you need a little peace and quiet).

Here's the good news: I promise that once you carve out some time to really assess what's working/not working and commit to investing energy and resources into rethinking your space to fully work for and not against you, the results will be mind-blowing, mind-altering, and mind-restoring.

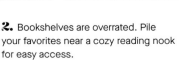

1. Want your deposit back? Skip the nails and use tape for cool, lo-fi vibes.

2. Bookshelves are overrated. Pile your favorites near a cozy reading nook for easy access.

3. Ceiling mounts are a drag to install. Hang lightweight plants on a curtain rod instead.

How Dysfunction Kills Mental Wellness

Design will always be an inextricably linked combination of form and function, so the *minute* it stops functioning the way it needs to is when, by definition, it becomes *dys*functional (thereby making its form kind of pointless). And here, my friends, is the precise moment poor design choices start to take a toll on your wellness.

You may be thinking, "So my medicine cabinet is a little messy. Big deal." But **home design is always a set of micro-domino effects** that make up the environment you interact in and with every day. (Or death by a thousand poorly designed paper cuts if done badly.) Setting up your home to take stuff *off* your plate (even if it's one less Q-tip to pick up off the floor) is a win. Take it.

Exhibit A:

THE MESSY AF MED CABINET

STATS

NICKNAME: The AM/PM Nightmare

BACKSTORY: The first thing you see in the morning is the last place you thought to organize.

EVAL: If only eight things fall out into the sink, it's a good day. (So, yeah, it's time.)

THE KICKER: Even if you did get up on the right side of the bed in the morning, a tumbling cascade of toothpaste, ibuprofen, and Q-tips will negate that. Fewer reasons to be annoyed in the morning will always be good for your mental wellness.

Exhibit B:

THE WFH ROOM THAT'S NSFW

STATS

NICKNAME: The Productivity Murderer

BACKSTORY: Ever-changing (and Zoom-appropriate) workplace demands called for a less-than-ideal, makeshift workplace setup to happen stat.

EVAL: If s*** can't get done comfortably, calmly, and confidently, it's officially what we call Not Working.

THE KICKER: Not being able to be productive leads way too easily into shame, disappointment, and (you guessed it) *more* unproductive mental spirals.

Exhibit C:

THE UN-PREPPY KITCHEN

STATS

NICKNAME: The No-Prep Zone

BACKSTORY: Countertops are an endangered species here. Good healthy food? We don't know her.

EVAL: Anything that makes eating/making/preparing good food difficult is an automatic no-go.

THE KICKER: Having people over is most likely going to be tough (Mental Wellness Killer alert). But, also, your health is holistic: Nourishing your body is also good for your mind. The harder that is to do, the worse it is for your overall health.

Exhibit D:

THE POKY PERENNIAL

STATS

NICKNAME: The Potted Terror

BACKSTORY: The corner next to the door seemed like a cute spot for a plant at first, but your cut-up ankles (and the I'm-only-making-one-trip grocery bags that keep knocking it down) beg to differ.

EVAL: Your arteries, water pipes, and high-traffic areas—all places that need to be clear of blockages.

THE KICKER: Softer plants might get a pass, but if the leaves are stiff and spiky (I mean, it's even called a snake plant—the warning is in the name), you really kind of had it coming. Ins and outs should be smooth sailing (read: as least annoying as possible).

Exhibit E:

THE OVERSTUFFED STORAGE CLOSET

STATS

NICKNAME: Just-Throw-It-in-Here-for-Now

BACKSTORY: In a pinch, it was your catchall for last-minute guest cleanups and unsightly appliances, but now it's become a legit black hole of god-knows-what.

EVAL: Try opening the door. (Mm-hmm, we rest our case, your honor.)

THE KICKER: Imagine the storage space you'd free up (and all the lost items you'd find) by rolling up your sleeves and tackling one area. If you're in the market for a shoe closet, extra pantry, appliance butler, backstock organizer—or, better yet, all of the above—pour yourself a drink, turn on a podcast, and get your deep clean on.

Subtle Signs That
Something Isn't Functioning

Saying no to poorly functioning design usually requires a mix of both physical and emotional labor on your part (which is why we often put it off). That bulky dresser you've been dying to get rid of? A physical hassle. Your first clarinet from band camp that's kinda broken, kinda not? An emotional negotiation. So often, dysfunction is hard to spot after a while because, over time, we get so used to living in it that we stop seeing it. When we eventually realize that we've been bending over backward to accommodate—even exacerbate— poor design, it's quite literally life-changing. Here are a few more telltale signs that something in your home needs to be confronted.

1. **There's an underlying dread.** If you feel that "ugh" in your bones every time you have to deal with it, that's probably a sign that there's something to confront—whether it's a whole room or a smaller spot somewhere (that corner in the garage you've been neglecting). Procrastination, thy name is usually Dysfunction I Don't Want to Face.

2. **There's a backstory.** Disclaimers are dangerous. Ever find yourself feelings embarrassed at having to explain how something works? ("Oh, yeah, the microwave handle is a bit wonky. We keep trying to superglue it and it won't stick")—bingo. It's probably something to address.

3. **There are extra steps.** Mind you, these steps are invisible to you because they've been folded into your daily routine for so long that you don't even question them anymore. ("You gotta use both hands and press it real hard to get it to work.")

JUMP AHEAD ➤

For more tips on how to get rid of stuff, check out my decluttering tips on page 111.

Looks Matter (in Design)

Don't get me wrong: Functional design can—and should—look amazing. (And let's be real: It's me you're talking to! You don't get emotional at my *QE* reveals for nothing.) Beauty inherently serves an important function in our lives. (Remember: Maximizing your quality of life means that if, at any given point along the way, you can afford to buy some measure of happiness—in this case, in the form of pieces that you love/make you happy/are cute AF—you absolutely should.)

Ideally, you want to strive for the best of both worlds. So I give you Exhibit A: The Highly Functional, Highly Gorgeous Coffee Corner.

1. Stick to a limited color palette (here, it's warm woods and rose-toned copper) for a streamlined, elevated look.

2. Form meets function in the best way when you keep items uniform both in style and in the way you store them.

The ~~Finishing~~ *Functional* Touches

Sometimes, you can't see the dysfunction through the design. While I'm all for gorgeous styling, in the end it'll just be for show unless you're setting up the space to function IRL—this includes accounting for traffic flow patterns, ideal/desired behavior, and activities (Will you be sitting for long periods? Will you need some range of movement? If so, how much?), all the way down to what time of day you'll be using the space and the amount of storage you'll need around it. Pinterest is a fantastic place to find inspiration and gather ideas for a project—just make sure you're doing a pass for the specific way your space needs to function for you and you're golden.

1. Storage ottomans are my favorite, functional twofer—perfect as comfy, extra seating for guests and for stashing away extra blankets and accessories.

2. Round side tables have fewer corners to bump into (and also double as extra seating in a pinch).

3. Make sure there's at least 15 inches between the coffee table and the edge of your sofa to ensure optimal space for passing through, scooching around people's legs, landing your drink on, and—my personal favorite—that well-deserved propping up of your feet after a long day.

Chapter 2
The Good Bits

Designing is planning. Period.

Function and form are the building blocks
of good design; lead with function because
form will always follow.

Optimizing for function results in a space that is
awesome for your mental wellness because your home
will save you time, minimize pain, mitigate stress,
and take extra work off your plate.

THE
Kitchen
SHOULD BE YOUR

Sous-Chef

Food is quite literally life.

It's our fuel, our gas, and universally what brings people together. So the kitchen—the place where you make, eat, and gather around food—needs to be designed to make anything and everything related to food easy. When you're not taking care of your body, that 100 percent affects your mind. The more of a nuisance it is to prepare good food, the less you'll do it (and the less healthier you'll be). The kitchen can also be one of the first rooms to get out of hand when things start to go haywire, and with good reason—it's one of the busiest rooms in the house! We all need to eat, so we're all in there at some point during the day. And depending on what season of life you're in, the kitchen may have needed to adapt to become your survival mode headquarters.

Whether it's now an eat-and-run station, a kid-focused snack pit stop, a hangout while you're microwaving leftovers (hey, I love a good leftovers meal!)—the point is that all of this is totally normal and okay. That's why making time periodically to reevaluate how the space is working for you is key. Since the kitchen is a high-function, high-traffic room, it's important to put it through the ringer once in a while. Treat this like an evaluation report you have to fill out for one of your employees (after all, your rooms should work *for* you and your wellness, amirite?).

To **YOU**

From **YOUR MENTAL WELLNESS**

Subject **Yearly Kitchen Eval Report**

It's that time again! Attached is the original job description for your kitchen. Remember: The three key attributes of a functional kitchen are (1) visibility, (2) convenience, and (3) community.

Thanks!

SOUS-CHEF

JOB DESCRIPTION

REPORTS TO: Head Chef (YOU)

ROLES AND RESPONSIBILITIES:
- Facilitate the making of good, healthy food at all times
- Make food prepping a cinch
- Keep everything easily accessible in any given spot
- Ensure a smooth workflow to minimize traffic
- **Most Important: Keep Head Chef inspired, calm, supported, and happy**

REQUIREMENTS:
- Must be organized AF
- Must be a multitasking profesh
- Must remain cool as a cuke under pressure

NICE-TO-HAVES:
- Space to chow down
- Ability to entertain/host

YOUR WELLNESS, INC.

THE WELLNESS *audit*

The Everything-Including-the-Kitchen-Sink Test

Let's get reacquainted with your kitchen. Evaluations are a great time to look at things with fresh eyes and make honest assessments about what's working and not working. With a high-use room like a kitchen especially, it's easy to stop "seeing" things (clutter, appliances that fell out of favor, inconvenient setups). Now you can pinterest gorgeous kitchen photos all day long (and, boy, do I love a great Pinterest sesh! There's so much inspiration out there), but what I want to help you do is not only troubleshoot for function but also intentionally aim for a wellness-forward setup. Even if you don't have room in your budget for a full reno, a wellness-minded kitchen is 100 percent achievable by carving out a few hours, rolling up your sleeves, and tweaking just a few key things.

THE GOLDEN (SHELF) RULE

Supermarkets use the term *golden shelf* to refer to the shelf right at eye level (where they place the items they most want to sell us). Your fridge has a golden shelf, too—it's the one that's the easiest to see, reach, and grab from. Stock it with food you want to eat more of and relegate stuff you want to avoid everywhere else.

OUT OF SIGHT, OUT OF MIND
Keep foods you want to avoid behind closed cabinet doors— some studies suggest we eat 20 percent of food just because it's visible.

CLEAN FAST
Viewing a chaotic environment subconsciously could elicit "out-of-control" feelings, so prioritize a quick cleanup after meals.

SEE GREEN, EAT GREEN
Researchers have found that seeing greenery in the kitchen encourages the consumption of green foods.

YOUR KITCHEN, BUT MAKE IT BOUGIE
Making your kitchen feel like an upscale restaurant (muted color palette, minimalist styling) could help you eat more mindfully.

THE KITCHEN SHOULD BE YOUR SOUS-CHEF

KITCHEN MATHEMATICS

Not having enough workspace to prep food is kind of a buzzkill (and will prevent you from wanting to make anything at all). I've said it before and I'll say it again: **The way a space is designed affects your behavior.** If something's even a little bit inconvenient, you won't want to do it (and most likely won't end up doing it). Annoyance is the foolproof precursor to a cascade of choices that can turn into a mental wellness disaster. If you don't have enough counter space, here are a few creative counteroffers (see what I did there?).

➕ add: SURFACES

Stovetop

Sinktop

Makes clean up easy!

➖ subtract: COUNTERTOP CLUTTER

Stash

Hang

Hello, clear countertops!

DIVIDE + CONQUER

1. identify spots that get all the action.

2. reserve prime real estate—areas that are literally within arm's reach.

3. stock the key items you need.

AVOID TRAFFIC JAMS

Chart out frequent "user paths" (the walk to the trash can, the stove-to-sink route) to maximize efficiency and minimize annoyance.

CLEANING SUPPLIES GO HERE

THE CLEANING SPOT

COFFEE STUFF GOES HERE

SPICES GO HERE

THE COOKING SPOT

THE COFFEE SPOT

THE POWER OF one

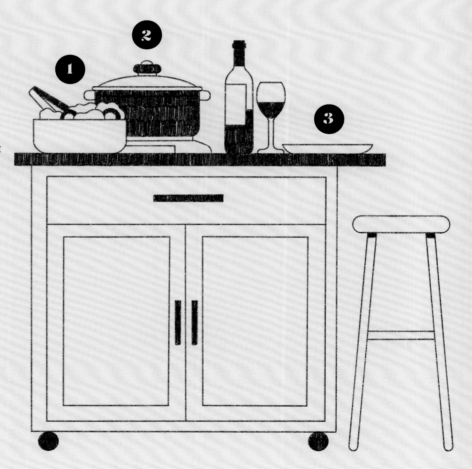

When space is severely limited, the right kitchen cart is a great investment. With a butcher board countertop, strategic storage throughout, and an overhang (for easy sitting), it's the do-it-all station that keeps your transitions seamless (and the drinks bottomless).

1. prep
CHOP / SEASON / KNEAD

2. cook
WARM / MIX / MASH

3. eat
DRINK / NOSH / GRAZE

PUT YOUR KITCHEN TO THE *test*

daily use

Use Frequency: Mid to High
Visibility: High

The most popular items go on the lowest shelves. Graduate the rest by usage, with the least used pieces all the way at the tippy top.

constant use

Use Frequency: High
Visibility: High

Anything you reach for multiple times a day should be out in the open or stored in your topmost drawers.

occasional use

Use Frequency: Low
Visibility: Low

Bulky appliances, serve-ware, and other once-in-awhile pieces should be behind closed doors to keep maximize your counter space.

THE ARM'S REACH
quiz

1.

✓ Can I reach this?

Not all arms are created equal, so make sure you adjust and customize your hot spots to meet your own reach.

2.

✓ Can others reach this?

In a multiperson household, strategic placement is key: Keep specific items easily reachable for its users to encourage independence.

3.

✓ Can we all reach things without crashing into one another?

Make sure you establish zones to minimize traffic jams during rush hour.

A++

Plan your kitchen by zone

THE KITCHEN SHOULD BE YOUR SOUS-CHEF

WORK-LIFE
balance

or How I Learned
to Love Not
Eating at My Desk

Get that blood flowing, do a few stretches, and take a stand (literally). We are all sitting waaaay too much as it is. If you have to make it a quick one, a meal or snack break taken standing could help divide the day. Carving out a dedicated space for an activity signals to you that it's important and worth your undivided attention. Listen, I probably sound quaint telling you to do this in the age of "Netflix and eat in front of your screen," but being mindful and present in all areas of your life is nonnegotiable when it comes to your mental health.

Get up off of that thing

WELLNESS TIP

When possible, try to use proper dinnerware and flatware over paper and plastic. Not only is it better for the environment, but it's also another detail that encourages you to eat more mindfully and understand eating as an act of self-care that warrants dignity.

MINDFUL EATING | BEST PRACTICES

notice.

Think not just about taste but also about texture, temperature, and overall sensation of the food in your mouth as you're chewing.

go slow.

Don't gulp it down—notice the subtle transition from chewing to swallowing.

reflect.

What did you notice while you were chewing? When did what you're eating lose flavor? What's unique about its texture?

THE DINING ROOM SHOULD BE YOUR *maître d'*

If you do have a formal dining room, it should function like a solid, senior-level waitstaff assigned to a large group—an attentive team of service-minded pros whose sole job is to keep the food coming and the drinks flowing (shout-out to these massively essential workers, amirite?). The general area in your home (could be a room, could be a corner, could be a spot at your countertop near the booze!) where you gather to eat, drink, and connect with loved ones should do the exact same thing. Which is why—after your table and seating options—the two hardest-working pieces in any given dining room are the sideboard cabinet (other versions of this piece are called a buffet or credenza) and—one of my personal favorites when it comes to dining room workhorses—the bar cart.

WELLNESS TIP

Pieces like this taller sideboard make impromptu gatherings super streamlined and easy to plan. Remember: Connecting with people over a meal is kind of a massive love fest for your health—you're getting physical nourishment and human connection at the same time (the best twofer).

A self-serve drink station is a huge bear hug for your guests, no? Bonus: It relieves some of your hosting duties since your guests can just help themselves all night long.

No bar cart? No problem. Set up a minibar with a tray to wrangle all your items.

3

Clear Your Space, Clear Your Mind

What you see is literally what your mind gets.

Home organization is a window to your soul.

I can tell a lot about someone by the way their home is or isn't organized. And listen: This isn't about passing judgment on anyone's home habits—we all get busy! Even the most organized person can unravel and our homes are one of the first places we see evidence of that. It's a bit of a catch-22 because **disorganization is both a symptom and a cause of poor mental wellness.** What I've found is that getting ahead of it as much as you can by setting up (and maintaining!) some organizational structure in the home has tangible positive effects—at the very least, you're doing what you can to create a more manageable, day-to-day life. (And let's be honest: Don't we all want that?)

Remember: What you take in with your eyes gets on an express train straight to your nervous system and your brain (aka your body's HQ). **What you see is literally what your mind gets.** So you *must* be ruthless about what you allow into it.

Outside of things you can't control—the view through your windows, basic floor plans if you're not in the market for major changes, furniture that has to stay put for the time being— **everything you see in your home is a choice you've made.** And if it's disorganized, counterproductive, or more to visually process than you need to, you're basically letting cortisol (your stress hormone) live rent-free in your head, body, and soul. And I don't know about you, but the absolute last thing I need in my life is more stress!

Enter organization.

Now don't worry: This chapter isn't going to be yet another person in your life nagging you to clean (though you may feel the urge to roll up your sleeves and do so, and, if you do, don't say I didn't warn ya!). What we're going to do is unpack organization itself; the real reason it's so hard to get ourselves to do it and why it's often a symptom of deeper, inner challenges you may be facing. Will there be gorgeous photos of organized homes in the mix? Hell yes. But will there also be a deeper dive into the mental wellness benefits of organized living? Also, yes.

I'm incredibly passionate about organization—I learned from my own circuitous personal journey that **organizing what you see right in front of you is sometimes all you've got.** You might be facing a mountain of problems in pretty much all areas of your life, and all of them could be completely out of your control, but taking a deep breath and rearranging your sock drawer could literally be a lifeline (because you're bringing order and control to *something*). It sounds inconsequential, but it's really not—it's everything.

It's your home, your rules. Change is possible because you've got all the power. **Your home should work for you—let's hold it accountable.**

What *is* organization?

Before you throw money at the Container Store, let's break it down.

Organizing is the act of creating a functional system. Does that sound scary? Don't worry, I promise you it's not! Because the truth is, *anything* can be a system. (If you keep extra shampoo under your sink, that's a system! Now, if every time you pull out a bottle, you knock down your water-floss device, that system could probably use a rethink.) When it comes to a home, you can regard it as a bunch of smaller systems (bathroom storage is its own set of systems, the kitchen is another, etc.) that all ladder up to one massive system that essentially keeps your home running. And since your home should—first and foremost—work *for* you and the way you want to live your life, what you're really doing when you're organizing is you're building a kind of personal infrastructure— *you're creating a system of living that works for you.*

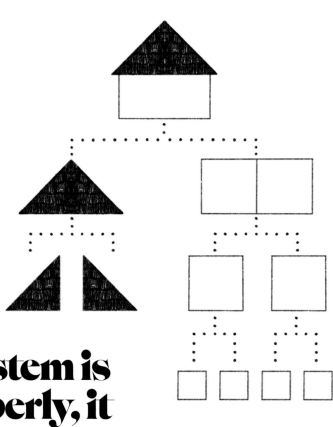

When a system is set up properly, it provides order, sets up a process, and establishes rules.

IF ONLY IT WERE THIS EASY

BEFORE

I know, I know—I couldn't resist! (What can I say—I like to give the people what they want.) But listen: To get from Point A to Point B, there are some key steps in between (including, yes, making the tough decisions re: what to get rid of), and I'm going to walk you through all of it. In fact, I like to eat my veggies first, so what's say we take out the trash first before we get to some more eye candy?

This is where we're gonna get down and dirty. You in?

AFTER

It's All Gonna Be Okay

Here's the good news: You're about to clear out space for the life you *really* want to live. Congratulations! I seriously couldn't be more happy for you. Depending on where you're at, this could be the Great Clean of the Century (in which case, grab your garbage bags), or this could be tackling a few spots you've been avoiding around the house (yep, we've alllll got those). Either way, I've got tips and advice for everyone. I personally love cleaning (yes, I'm one of those! C'mon, you've seen *Queer Eye*, you know how I roll) and believe that a good clean-out is a step you absolutely, at all costs, cannot skip when organizing a home.

Start small.

Like, I mean really small. Embarrassingly small. So small that you really won't have any excuse not to do it. Studies show that when you set your goals too high, you are way less likely to even get started because you've most likely mismatched the goal with your current capacity/ability/resources. Maybe the dreaded junk drawer feels too overwhelming right now (more on that later!). Or maybe that corner in the garage you can't bring yourself to make eye contact with just isn't going to happen this weekend. Listen: If the only thing you can get yourself to do is tackle that one teeny-tiny problematic spot on that middle shelf in your bathroom medicine cabinet where the toothpaste keeps getting knocked over, I'm telling you—that moment of zen you get from F-I-N-A-L-L-Y figuring out how to make it work for you should not be minimized. One less thing for you to be annoyed about is ONE LESS THING. It counts. It matters. It's worth it.

Make it fun.

Turn on a podcast or your favorite playlist. (Music has a proven positive effect on your mood! So if cleaning stresses you out, try to work yourself up to it by blasting some of your favorite tunes and having a quick little dance party to shake out the scaries.) Pour yourself a drink (or two). Turn on some reruns (watching something you're familiar with helps soothe anxiety). Order food. Plan to reward yourself after you reach a certain point. Even though, yes, cleaning is technically a chore, there's no reason it has to *feel* like one!

111

Take it easy.

Cleaning can dredge up feelings you weren't prepared for. If you get emotional about something, allow yourself to get emotional. If you need a moment, take a moment. If you need a break, take a break. Do what you need to do to get through one full sesh and don't forget to pat yourself on the back when you're done.

Also: It's okay if you can't make some decisions on the spot! You can always revisit items in the next round. Decision fatigue is real: It exhausts your executive function, so if it helps to hang on to a few things until you're more ready to let them go or have more energy to address in the next go-round, that's totally okay.

Keep reminding yourself that, in the end, you're doing this to make your space work better for you.

AND WHEN ALL ELSE FAILS . . . PHONE A FRIEND

If you're struggling to make decisions about older items (clothes and shoes especially), having a second opinion around will help keep the momentum going! Pick someone who loves you (duh), who knows you pretty well, and preferably someone you can stand being around for a minute because cleaning can take a while and gets, well, messy (ironically). Your mom might be helpful to a degree (God bless all mothers), but if you want to gently strangle her after ten minutes, she may not be good for your mental state while tackling a deep clean.

Asking for help is also a great way to keep yourself accountable—studies show that telling others about your goals makes it more likely that you'll make them happen. So think of it as accountability IRL, in real time.

Don't Throw It Away

No, you're not off the hook here! Anything broken beyond repair or not worth the cost of repair (or your very valuable time) should still be tossed. But there are tons of other ways to give items new life that don't involve taking up space in your home.

➤ MAKE A DONATION

In addition to thrift stores (you can schedule a pickup if you don't have time to drive!), look up local libraries, schools, and smaller businesses that might be in the market for some donated pieces.

➤ MAKE A TRADE

Plan a style swap with friends (a great way to keep each other accountable if everyone is due for a clean-out). Bring your unwanted pieces—and wine—and voilà! You've got yourself a sustainable, free stuff par-tay.

➤ MAKE SOME CASH

There are lots of online outlets where you can make some extra cash off still-usable pieces! (See page 296 for my favorites.) Yes, it'll take some work (creating listings, taking photos, managing inquiries), but it's a great solve if you're having trouble letting go.

➤ MAKE IT NEW

Get your DIY on. From flipping to repurposing (even in your own home!), give new life to your pieces that you don't want to part with by reimagining them somewhere else/used another way.

Check in with Yourself

Sorting through your stuff can get emotional. Emotions arise to tell you something or incite some kind of action that's needed. It's important to be able to name the emotion so you can then figure out how to respond.

Emotional Warning Signs

If you pick up an item and you feel one or more of the following, it's a good sign that this item needs a rethink at the very least (and potentially a full-on removal at the most). The rule of thumb is **immediacy:** If it's not something you're going to get to at this stage in your life and it isn't an urgent need, keep it out of sight until you're ready to deal with it. Key feelings to monitor include:

- **Guilt**
- **Shame**
- **Regret**
- **Stress**
- **Annoyance**
- **Something that makes you feel "stuck"**
- **Something that reminds you of someone toxic**
- **Something that reminds you of a version of yourself you've outgrown**

Your Junk Drawer? Handled.

We're doing it.
It's happening.

A drawer (any drawer, really—it doesn't have to be your official junk drawer, but it can be if you're game!) is a great bite-size gateway drug before jumping into a full-on organization bender because:

1. There's a clear light at the end of the tunnel. (I mean, would you look at that gorgeous photo down there?!)

2. It usually won't take more than a couple hours. (But if it ends up taking longer, do not panic. THIS IS OKAY.)

3. It's enough of an accomplishment to start building some momentum to keep you on a roll.

Use your iPhone boxes!

Choose Your Own Adventure

You can decide how far down the rabbit hole you want to go, depending on what you're up for, the state and location of your junk drawer, and how much time you've got.

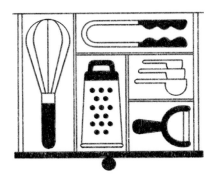

➤ LEVEL 1: **Reorganize**

This is the most common strategy *if* all the items in here are actually useful, needed, and convenient to have around. Once you've thrown away the actual junk and categorized what's left, just make sure your items are housed in the correctly sized sections and boom. Done and done.

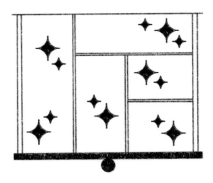

➤ LEVEL 2: **Redistribute**

A lot of junk drawers have items that actually belong elsewhere (tools, writing utensils, crafty things). What if you could eliminate your junk drawer altogether? Re-home the items where they actually belong and now you've got an extra drawer open for the taking. (You're welcome!)

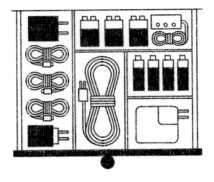

➤ LEVEL 3: **Rebrand**

The term *junk drawer* is intimidating—and often a misnomer—if the items in here *do* have a theme (Stationary Station, Charger Spot). Officially retire the Drawer Formerly Known As Junk and cement its new status—and name—in your home. (Bonus: Every time you refer to it, you'll be reminded of your hard work.)

Organizing what you see right in front of you is sometimes all you've got.

EXCUSES, EXCUSES

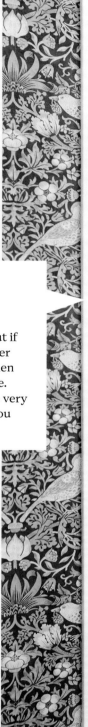

I Have Nothing to Wear!

You *do* have stuff to wear—but if all your favorite duds are either unreachable or unfindable, then they're effectively unwearable. Set up a system so that, at the very least, you don't forget what you actually own!

I'm Always Late!

No one is born a late person; they just have things that make them late along the way. Designate spots for all your stuff so that every time you need to leave the house, you're not triggering a chaotic keys/wallet/sunglasses search party.

I Have a Hard Time Focusing While Working from Home.

You might have too much clutter around you. If you don't feel productive when you sit down to work, a quick decluttering sesh might be in order.

Emotional Decluttering 101

Procrastination isn't about laziness, a lack of self-control, or being irresponsible; it reflects an **inability to manage negative emotions in the short term**, which is why organizing is so easy to put off. Items that bring up emotions like guilt, shame, anxiety, excessive sadness, and overwhelm need to be assessed and dealt with on a regular basis to make sure your home remains a place of rest, restoration, and calm. If every time you look at something it calls up emotions that slow you down, then it's worth having a conversation with yourself. If you're not going to be able to deal with something right away (a shelf you've been meaning to put up, a broken appliance), put it away—completely out of sight—for the time being. Focus on your current life, present goals, and the person you are right now.

A QUICK + DIRTY TIDY SESH

Here's how I'd edit this nightstand to streamline the mornings and optimize for sleep.

 NAY

Plants are great, but dealing with spiky, protruding leaves first thing in the morning when you're reaching for your phone or glasses? Hard pass.

 NAY

Work stuff? Nope, not by your bed. Stash this away or store in another room entirely.

 YAY

This lamp isn't tall enough to provide task lighting for reading in bed, but if you're optimizing for sleep, it's perfect—low, dim, and filtered. (For more tips on how to calibrate light intake for nighttime, go to page 242.)

 YAY

A great way to avoid looking at screens first thing in the morning is to use an old school clock (when in doubt, go analog).

THE MORAL OF THE STORY: It's Okay to Be Who You Are

Okay, so you thought you were going to be a serene, lavender-sniffing bookworm who tucks in under a silk eye mask and keeps romantic keepsakes by your bed. So what if you're actually a CBD gummy–chewing Kindle addict who prefers a diffuser and needs blue light glasses + nightguard real estate on your nightstand before nodding off? (Fun fact: When working with clients who struggle with clutter, I often mentally place items in what I like to call the **"I Thought I Was Going to Be This Person"** category.) I've learned that facing these sorts of issues about who you thought you were is a kind of emotional confrontation with yourself, but probably one you wouldn't have had otherwise because how would you have known, right? A lot of this self-knowledge has to come from trial and error and, in my experience, the best way to deal with this is to show yourself a little compassion, cut your losses/accept what you now know to be true about yourself, and move forward accordingly. There's a funny stubbornness in holding on to items that don't function for you, especially when you've spent your own money on them. The regret that comes with having shelled out cash for something you were wrong about is definitely understandable, but the point is this: **Never feel bad about adjusting your design to reflect who you really are.** Life is short, and one of the ways to make the most of it is to quickly readjust after learning new information about who you are and what makes you happy.

125

LIVE IN THE

↓

P R E S E N T

THE PAST STUFF

*"Oh, that? That's
from when . . ."*

. . . I was dating this person I am no longer dating.

. . . I was sure I was going to do this activity that I never ended up doing.

. . . I used to rock this style of clothing that I wouldn't be caught dead in today.

. . . I used to fit into a size I've deluded myself into thinking I will one day fit into again.

. . . I was given a gift that I didn't, don't, and will never totally love.

THE FUTURE STUFF

"One day I'll . . ."

. . . finish this home project I will never finish, even if you put a gun to my head.

. . . pick up this hobby I definitely won't pick up.

. . . read these books that I've totally lost interest in.

. . . hang this art that I actually deep down don't care a whole lot about.

. . . use these items I've been saving for a life I'm most likely not going to have but once thought I might.

Remember this:

What enters your eyes enters your mind.

The Mental Battleground of Trying to Get Rid of Things

Only the things that support and serve the life you're **currently** living deserve pride of place, thoughtful storage solutions, and your time and energy. What are your priorities and values right now? Keep only what is relevant to these. With the rest, you must fight the good fight.

The Self-Love **Angel** Says:

➤ Just because it has use left doesn't obligate you to keep it around!

➤ It's okay—you didn't know at the time that it wouldn't end up serving you. Forgive yourself for that.

➤ If you lack the skills/tools/know-how to complete the task in the next week, put it away for the time being.

The Toxic **Devil** Says:

➤ It may not have proven useful for you, but it still has use left.

➤ Ugh, but you spent $__ on it. You don't want that money to go to waste, do you?

➤ Once you learn how to [skills/tools/know-how you lack to complete the task], you'll get right to it.

127

A clean space feels inherently inviting. Just make sure all your favorite activities—games, eats— are ready to go.

Organizing Is Self-Care

Say your mantras and get your organizing on. Taking the time to set your home up to work optimally is an act of service—for you, by you.

Making something easy is a way of saying, This is important to me.

➤ ORGANIZATION TAKES STUFF OFF YOUR PLATE.

When you've got a lot going on, time spent looking for things you need can feel like an added strain. Good organization should make things insanely easy for you, whether it's reaching for a pen or reaching for the garlic salt.

➤ ORGANIZATION REDUCES STRESS.

Clutter has been linked to increased levels of cortisol—your stress hormone (yeah, not cool). So by removing clutter—whether it's by prioritizing closed storage systems or regularly cleaning out your stuff—you're literally decreasing stress.

➤ ORGANIZATION ENCOURAGES CONNECTION

Keeping things organized and ready for guests makes it harder to stay isolated. Remember: Having a strong network of loved ones you feel comfortable inviting over when you need support is crucial to your (mental) well-being.

Organization Speaks. Are You Listening?

An organized system tells you loud and clear that whatever is being organized is worth your time, energy, and consideration. It also tells you that all the various users of this organized system—and *their* comfort, energy, and joy—matter.

Making your joy easily accessible is important.

Your joy matters.

A clean, guest-ready home makes inviting people over easy.

Your emotional health matters.

Making things easy for everyone in your family is important.

Every member of your family matters.

Making it easy to get ready in the morning is important.

Your time matters.

I know, right? Listen, in a world full of distractions, your productivity (and mental wellness) will thank you if your workspace leaves you with zero excuses

Time-Savers Are Lifesavers

The Ultimate Guide to Drop Zones

Front-loading the work by taking time to organize something—anything—buys you time in the long run. And time is the only thing we have, really. If for nothing else than to buy you more time to focus on the things that matter, check out some of my favorite organizational tips for hot spots around the home.

➤ **THE FIVE-MIN ENTRYWAY FIX:**

Hooks for the win. Always.

THE FIVE-MIN BEDROOM FIX:

A storage-packed nightstand is the official MVP of any bedroom.

➤ THE FIVE-MIN HOME-OFFICE FIX:

The underrated clutter-wrangler, trays
always deliver and never disappoint.

THE ORGANIZATION ONE-SHEET

Whether you're strapped for time or just need a quick guide for how to think about cleaning and organizing, these three rules will help anyone organize anything in no time. I promise you that if you follow these four pillars, your home will turn into a mind-calming place that supports where and who you are right now.

1. BE INTENTIONAL. Carefully consider what you choose to leave visible (these should be thought-through, curated items that evoke your happiness or are in consistent use).

2. BE UNIFORM. Using identical containers where you can will give your eyes less to process, which will lead to less stress!

3. PRIORITIZE THE PRESENT. Decide what's needed for immediate use as opposed to what you need to store away for later (such as seasonal items).

Chapter 3
The Good Bits

A disorganized home can be both a symptom and a cause of poor mental wellness.

Organizing something is a way of saying *this matters*.

What you choose to keep in your home should support who you really are in the present and where you're really at right now.

Kids' Spaces

(AKA THE SURVIVAL GUIDE FOR PARENTS)

(for the design stuff, not the actual parenting — just to be clear)

TO ALL PARENTS EVERYWHERE: First and foremost, I salute you. You have bravely, selflessly, and perhaps even reluctantly at times (hey, no judgment here, parenting is hard AF) taken on the enormous task of raising the next generation of humans who will (hopefully) become inclusive, empathic, and kind adults. This is by no means an easy feat, and I have nothing but the utmost respect and appreciation for the incredible responsibility you shoulder day in and day out.

As meaningful and beautiful as it is, parenting can also be excruciatingly stressful, exhausting, and at times can feel damn near impossible. And I want you to know—Uncle Bobby is here to help! Consider this section of the book my way of wrapping an army blanket around you and handing you a canteen of ~~water~~ whiskey. Because listen—I've worked with tons of parents and their little ones, and the biggest takeaway for me is this: Design tends to be severely underutilized when it comes to kids' spaces. Like, severely. Forgoing good design for kids is almost like having a free babysitter who's always around but is never asked to help. (Okay, maybe that's a bit of a stretch.) From impractical storage solutions to loads of unused closet space to suboptimal color palettes and everything in between—I've worked

through it all and have seen the real effects of what a functional, beautiful kid space can do for a parent's mental health (and the kid's, whether they know it or not).

Here's my PSA: As a society, if we aren't prioritizing the mental wellness of parents everywhere, we risk the entire next generation of humans being half-realized products of strained parenting. I for one refuse to stand by and let that happen. As a designer, the best gift I can give you is all my design advice for how to optimize the space these smaller humans live in. Happy kid, happy parent. But also: happy parent, happy kid. It's a two-way happiness street, and I'm here for it.

TOY-POCALYPSE?

~~HANDLED.~~

HERE'S THE THING: Kids are small but the amount of stuff they have is, well, NOT small. In fact, the smaller the kid, the more stuff they have. Fact: Even their toys have toys. Kids everywhere are adorable clutter magnets, clutter creators, and clutter bringers (the sheer amount of stuff they acquire *outside* the home that then makes its way *into* your home is kind of insane). This is largely because play is extremely important for kids—it's how their brains literally develop and learn. Now, if only this key part of early childhood development didn't mean wading through a grade A toynado in your house most days. Making cleanup easy to maintain (and, dare I say, even fun) is the key to having your little ones take

part in it. Removing even a little bit from your plate is a win, amirite? And because clutter has been linked to increased stress, it's my belief (and experience!) that dealing with

clutter—and designing storage that allows kids to help corral their own clutter—is a huge way design can support a parent's *and* child's mental wellness.

uncle bobby says

Keep storage low to the ground so it's easier for kids to put things away. **BONUS:** This is also great for kids (or adults!) with special needs—always optimize for independence for everyone across the board.

Color Coordinated

Organizing by color is easy on the eyes— and easy to teach (start 'em young).

For Readers

Got kids who can read? Get your label maker and put 'em to work.

Clear Winners

Clear storage means no questions asked— everything is in plain sight.

Go Custom

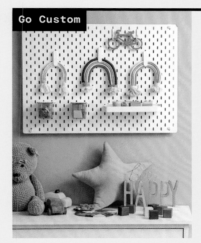

Some toys are snowflakes. I get it. Customized storage is worth it, trust me.

STRESS REDUCER #461:
THE NOT-SO-SECRET SECRET WAY TO PURGE

Keep some stuff you know they don't play with in the garage or other storage spots outside of their rooms. If they look for it, you can show them that you haven't thrown it away. If they don't end up missing it, you're in the clear to toss. **PRO TIP:** This works for the adults in your house, too.

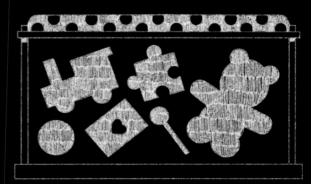

145

HOW TO WIN THE BATTLE ROYALE: DISPLAY VS. PUT AWAY

There's an art to figuring out which items deserve pride of place. Of course, whichever one makes your kid inordinately happy usually makes the first cut in terms of display. But there's also size/shape (since some items are just impossible to store neatly, displaying them somewhere is really the only option) and the

very real, very important aspect of eye-sore-ness (real talk: your mental wellness involves minimizing pain). Listen, just because that Hulk action figure is that exact shade of vomit-triggering green you hate doesn't make you a bad parent.

Strategic display tactics can also help shine a light on some forgotten toys that haven't seen the light of day in a while (say hello to that new toy feeling without the price tag), and also encourage play in a specific direction if you're needing an assist (are we not loving veggies? Let's have our veggie toys out!).

uncle bobby says

Toys on display can function as visual reminders (kind of like merchandise in a store!). You may not have room for EVERY American Girl doll to be in full view, but if you have one styled in plain sight, that's enough to remind you that there are more in the drawers below.

JUST SAY NO
(TO THE KIDS' SECTION)

One of the biggest stressors that comes attached to having kids is the massive financial weight. To ease that burden just a bit, invest in more neutral, versatile pieces that grow with your kid so you can use them longer. (Plus, non-eyesore design for kids = less pain for the adults = mental wellness booster. It's a win-win all around.)

ONE TABLE. THREE STAGES. Pieces that grow with your kids mean three things: (1) neutral, (2) versatile, and (3) adjustable.

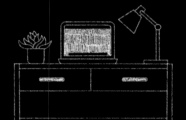

FUNCTIONAL DESIGN FOR ALL

For kiddos with specific needs and sensitivities, it's important to make a few tweaks to their bedroom to make sure they're set up for success. While the full design plan should be worked through with your healthcare professional (as every kid will require a customized setup based on his/her/their specific challenges), I've found the adjustments below to be a great starting point. Everyone, no matter what their situation, deserves to be in a space that has been thought through to help minimize frustration, maximize happiness, and enhance their wellness.

Opt for a generally minimal setup (e.g., rug tassels can catch on things like wheels) to allow better access to the room.

Install blackout curtains and paint rooms in calming hues for children who see color and light more intensely.

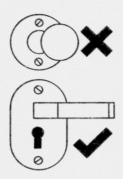

Lever door handles make for easier maneuvering.

Motion-sensor lights eliminate the hassle of lamps, switches, and knobs.

MY FAVORITE KID-FRIENDLY NEUTRAL BASES:

Girls are pink, boys are blue? I'm over the limiting color choices, aren't you?

NEUTRALITY
IS BEAUTIFUL

Super-bright colors can be too stimulating for a bedroom, especially for kids. With that being said, you definitely still want some playful touches. The best way to stretch out design choices for longer (read: save money!) is to use more soothing, neutral-toned hues as your base color while adding accents and pops in brighter colors. That way, you can switch out your accents as your kids grow.

THE SOOTHING-BUT-NOT-SNOOZY WAY TO DESIGN A BABY ROOM

No, this isn't a rule against anything bright, colorful, or fun! This is a call to take a step back and, as much as possible, optimize your kid's space for the #1 activity that needs to go on in there: sleep. Since *their* sleep is tied to *your* sleep, at all costs (the biggest one being your mental wellness), the design in this room should say "let's go night-night" over "let's play." This means creating an overall soothing, calming environment for all five senses. Even if your kid's bedroom still has books and toys, good design can keep things zoned and organized.

uncle bobby says

Be mindful of what's in the kid's line of sight when they're in bed! A reading nook (or even a chill lineup of stuffed animals) is potentially a more calming sight for a kid who's tucked in and ready for bed versus an action figure setup or a colorful bank of markers and crayons.

PARENTS, TAKE A BOW
(AND THEN TAKE A SEAT)

Self-care is not selfish. But when your little ones are extra little, going somewhere and shutting the door might not be an option. (Even if your kids are older, this may not always be possible.) "Small" things like an insanely comfy chair that rocks (both literally and figuratively) can make the difference between losing it and making it through the day.

149

4

Coming to Your Senses

Design is, by definition, something we can make sense of only by way of our senses. So when you start to plan out a space, considering how each of your senses will experience the room is a great starting point.

Being aware of how your senses respond to your environment is also a huge pillar of mindfulness, and staying present is a super-important muscle to develop if you struggle with anxiety or if you're committed to maintaining your mental wellness in general.

When I first learned about mindfulness—a form of meditation and general mindset focused on being fully in the present moment, deeply aware of and nonjudgmental regarding one's own thoughts and feelings—it really made a lot of sense to me. Staying fully present in the now is an active choice not to ruminate or worry about the future (anxiety) or stay stuck and/or debilitated by the past (depression).

As a designer, one mindfulness technique in particular stood out to me: the **54321 method**. This is a grounding technique used in multiple types of therapy to help someone come down from a panic or anxiety attack by engaging all five senses. This exercise can be done literally anywhere and helps you stay in the present and in your body, an act that directly combats the panic, since racing, anxious thoughts keep you stuck in your head.

It struck me that interior design could be used as a tool here—**creating a sensory-rich environment at home could give you lots of visually interesting pieces, colors, and images to help keep you a bit more present.** (And, honestly, who isn't even a little bit more present in a well-designed space? That's kind of the whole point of good design, amirite?) Design is nothing if not a full, sensory experience. While I'm not at all saying that design can—or should—replace professional mental health treatment if you need it, what I am saying is that design can give you interesting stimuli to look at/smell/hear/touch to help ground you in the present moment.

So a cool-looking coffee table won't cure your depression, but it might give you something interesting to process in that moment (and for a busy, stressed, and chaotic mind, every moment of relief, no matter how small, counts). In some ways, **good design can function almost like an intentionally beautiful distraction.**

Bottom line: **Taking the time to think through each room of your house by way of each sense will ultimately help you create a fuller, more thoughtful experience in your home** with the added side effects of keeping you just a bit more present. And, in my experience, when it comes to mental wellness, *every* little bit counts.

LIST 5 THINGS YOU CAN **see**.

LIST 4 THINGS YOU CAN **touch**.

LIST 3 THINGS YOU CAN **hear**.

LIST 2 THINGS YOU CAN **smell**.

LIST 1 THING YOU CAN **taste**.

Keeping all your senses engaged helps keep you in the present.

THE FIVE SENSES

A LEGEND

Smell

Give your nose something to notice when you're taking deep, mindful breaths.

Hearing

You want to be just as mindful about what sounds you block out as you are about what you let in.

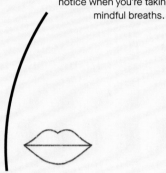

Taste

I'm skipping taste here, but I do believe in eating mindfully. For tips on how to design your mealtimes to help you stay present, jump back to page 90.

Touch

This one's a twofer: Not only do textural pieces encourage the act of touch, but they're also a treat for the eyes.

Sight

The two key things you want your eyes to do in a given space are (1) **focus** and (2) **move.** (Yes, good design can help your eyes do both!)

STAY FOCUSED
How to Design Around a Focal Point

In design, we understand that the eye actually *wants* to be guided, wants to be "told where to look." When you don't know where to look, your eyes naturally start scanning around, trying to figure out how to process what they're seeing. When design can help establish a sense of order—whether it's with one major focal point in a room or multiple, smaller focal points—your eyes actually "like" this because they don't have to do as much work.

Contrast for the Win

Why Our Eyes Love Contrast

The eye is naturally drawn to contrast because it stands out—the difference (in color, texture, shape, size) helps us make sense of what we're seeing faster. (That is, black handles on white cabinet doors make the handles easier to distinguish, making them even easier for our brains to process.) Incorporating some form of contrast is a tried-and-true way to not only anchor a space but also give your eyes a place to land when you walk into a room. When a room doesn't have even a *little* contrast, it can feel unintentional, bland, and "tiring" on the eyes because they have to do a bit more work to gather information. (What about monochromatic styles, you ask? Well, you can still create contrast through texture, which is personally one of my favorite ways to incorporate contrast!)

LEFT: An unexpected deep teal makes the wall art and glossy countertops pop (I love a little drama).

RIGHT: Neutral textiles against wood tones? Perfection.

Contrast helps our brains make sense of what we're seeing faster.

Velvet, leather, and wood, oh my. A
moody color palette with lots of textural
contrast keeps things interesting.

The coffee table's wood-grain markings in opposite directions function almost like stripes. That plus the zigzag rug pattern (which naturally leads your eyes to all the other black moments in the room), and you've got eye movement for days.

Keep It Moving

Why Good Design Always Encourages Eye Movement

In design, the goal is to keep your eyes engaged, aka moving around the room. This happens organically when the room has been thoughtfully arranged to direct your eyes to different areas within the space. (This also applies to smaller, styled moments like a beautifully styled bookcase or an interesting coffee table moment.) I do this in all kinds of ways when I'm designing a space—from the repetition of certain colors and patterns to the choice and placement of specific textures.

Angular lines everywhere you look: The chair profile and the graphic line art mimic each other, keeping your eyes engaged.

Customize Your Sound

Undoubtedly, there are lots of sounds in and around your home you can't control (appliances, kid noise, the city). Sound design for wellness is all about figuring out what you *can* control and calibrating both what enters your ears and what doesn't.

What You Hear at Home Matters

Sound On

To trigger the release of dopamine—your "feel good" brain chemical that helps regulate mood, pleasure, and feelings of reward/motivation—layer in music or nature sounds when you need a little stress relief. Studies also show that white/ambient noise can help you sleep at night. There are lots of beautiful, modern ways of incorporating sound design seamlessly into your home that feel intentional and work great for entertaining, too.

Sound Off

When it comes to disruptive noise, investing in good insulation if you're able to is great. But there are also easier and more cost-effective ways to help block out noise. Fabrics and furniture help slow sound waves, so try placing them strategically against walls to help soften noises. Plants also help absorb sound, so try styling larger ones near thinner walls and windows.

My Two Cents on Scents

Your Nose Knows More Than You Think

Smell is closely linked with memory and emotion. Think about how specific smells bring you right back to a place or time in your life (there's nothing like a whiff of Acqua Di Gio to take me right back to the '90s). Being intentional about the way your home greets you is a way of customizing the experience of your home from the moment you walk in the door. (This is also why I'm a big fan of having a signature scent for your home! It sends a powerful message—a familiar scent that makes you happy becomes linked with your home.) While some clinical studies link certain scents, like lavender, to effects like lower cortisol levels and better sleep, in my experience scents end up being really personal. So it's best to go with whatever you love and are drawn to. Personally, I love anything that smells woodsy and/or reminds me of being in nature—cedar and sandalwood are a few of my go-tos.

My biggest recommendation, though, is to go au naturel: Natural scents are not only super cost effective, but they're also 100 percent safe to inhale—and safe for the environment! (Many fragrance products are made with artificial and often harmful chemicals that usually aren't itemized clearly on labels, so to play it safe, I personally avoid them.) All in all, taking scent into consideration is something I never overlook when I'm setting up a space and is a detail that definitely helps keep you in the present (especially during a meditation sesh or any sort of general breathing or mindfulness exercise).

PRO TIP

Adding heat to natural ingredients is my favorite scent hack. Try simmering cloves, apple cider, or lavender on the stove, or hanging eucalyptus stems in the shower. The scent will fill the space in no time. The best part? It's 100 percent natural (and if it's something you already have in your home, 100 percent free).

Yes, You Can Touch It

Texture Is the Gift That Keeps on Giving

Layering in interesting textures throughout your home is another way of engaging your senses. Surfaces and finishes that are organic, visually interesting, and styled to contrast with one another are all ways of inviting and encouraging touch.

OPPOSITE: It's all in the mix. Throw pillows in all kinds of fun fabrics, a higher-pile rug, and subtler patterns like crosshatch linen make for one big happy texture party.

RIGHT, ABOVE: Soften "harder" textures like wicker and brass with woven blankets and rugs.

RIGHT: Texture 101: Nubby throw pillows are always appropriate.

Sensory Overload Is a Good Thing

Good Design Always Helps You Stay Present

1. A casual gallery wall (with a fun neon focal point) gives your eyes plenty to look at. BONUS: The tall plant and larger graphic print will help block out ambient noise from the next room.

2. Woven rugs are easy on the eyes and fun for your feet.

3. A treat for the nose and the eyes, thanks to its elegant, tapered shape.

4. When it comes to pillows, I have one rule: Go nuts. **PRO TIP:** Textures such as velvet and linen are pretty much foolproof.

Chapter 4
The Good Bits

Good design always engages all of your senses in beautiful, interesting ways, and that helps you stay present (which means good design is legitimately good for your mental health).

Think like a designer: Use focal points and contrast to keep your eyes moving, engaged, and anchored.

Texture is a two-for-one: It's both visual and tactile. Use it anywhere and everywhere.

Don't forget about sound design—carefully curate what goes in and stays out of your ears (and your mind).

Your nose knows more than you think—just keep things au naturel and you're good to go.

THE (BATHROOM)

Break Room

Imagine a space that *feels* like an actual break
(sans vending machines or a Ping-Pong table).

A proper break room should acknowledge the humanity of its users. That means thoughtful bathroom design should bring dignity to a space designated for, let's face it, a lot of undignified human activities. And while you may assume the bathroom is mainly for supporting bodily functions, your mind is literally a part of your body (that's why mental health is really just *health*). So when it comes to the bathroom, the rules are as follows:

HIT RESET

Prioritizing a therapeutic mindset (soothing colors and patterns) is a good rule of thumb, but if rich, vibrant hues or fun patterns are what resets you, go for it!

MINDFUL DESIGN

Your *mind* should feel like it's getting a legitimate break, too. That means beauty, cleanliness, and organization are all non-negotiables.

FUNCTION-FORWARD

This is a high-traffic, high-function room. So whatever goes on in here (whether it's a long, indulgent bath or a speedy, pre-Zoom shave sesh) should be easy AF.

Wish you were here, huh?

REMINDER

Going to the bathroom when you need to is a literal way of listening to your body. Sure, it's one of the easier cues (because when you gotta go, you gotta go), but it still counts.

Aaaaand here is your moment of zen.

Whether you're making a pit stop in between meetings, indulging in your thirty-seven-step skincare routine, or coaching your kiddo through another grueling teeth-brushing sesh, the bathroom should be equipped to handle it all without breaking a sweat. Picture the calm demeanor of your favorite yoga instructor, the organizational wizardry of the Container Store, and the storage capacity of that library from *Beauty and the Beast* all rolled into one seriously beautiful room that's just as easy on the eyes as it is on your psyche.

BATHROOM STORAGE CAN BE
sexy AF

It's not gonna feel like a break if it's a hot mess in here.

To bring more function back to this space, think about where you can strategically stuff your stuff. (Tip: Keep backstock or extras in a closet or another room if space is limited.)

WALL STORAGE

UNDER-SINK STORAGE

OVER-THE-DOOR STORAGE

IN-SHOWER STORAGE

ALL ARE WELCOME HERE

(Just wash your hands)

Figure out what activities you are going to do in the bathroom first. Then plan accordingly. (Smaller spaces and/or spaces that need to be shared by multiple people will be extra-limited, so stick with the absolute necessities—like dental accessories and a blow-dryer—and store the rest of your toiletries elsewhere to keep the bathroom as open as possible.)

PARDON OUR DUST

While Bobby Berk gives us a makeover

One last word of advice before we break . . .

It's always good to go into a redesign knowing (and fully accepting) that there may be some trial and error. Outside of complete renos, bathrooms are often the most limited space in the home. You usually have to work with what you've got. That means some things might work, others might not, and it'll take some jiggering (and rejiggering) to get everything organized and styled the way you want to. This is okay!

And if you need an actual mental wellness break outside of a bathroom break, take it. Because when your body hurts, you rest it, right? Well, when your mind hurts, you have to rest it, too.

No, SERIOUSLY— take a *real* break →

☐ Get up.
☐ Do a quick body scan.
☐ Stretch.
☐ Go outside.
☐ Be in nature.
☐ Eat something.

☐ Move your body.
☐ Do a guided meditation. Deep breath in, loooong breath out. (Do that four more times.)
☐ Dance it out.
☐ Clean something.
☐ Hug someone.
☐ Tunes on and tune out.
☐ Off screen and in person.
☐ Laugh.
☐ Then laugh some more.

5

The Language of Color

MAKE IT SIMPLE,
BUT SIGNIFICANT

***

DON DRAPER

Being fluent in color is an incredibly powerful tool for mental wellness.

When I first started out as a designer, I approached color purely on instinct. (Remember: My blue curtain moment was 100 percent visceral—I was way too young to know anything about the science behind colors!) To me, colors always felt kind of like mood whisperers—subtle messengers that inexplicably, strangely, but undeniably told me to feel one way or another.

After working with countless clients over the years, I found out that this is actually a pretty common experience. Often, we're not consciously clocking what the colors of a space are telling us because the messages are being registered at the subconscious level—in our nervous system, in our brain, in our feelings. I learned later that chromotherapy is an actual thing (I knew I wasn't crazy!)—a whole field with tons of research and studies dedicated to testing the effects of color on behavior, mood, and wellness IRL.

Now I've got lots of advice about how to pick the right color palettes based on this stuff (and we're going to get into it all in this chapter), but keep in mind that my foolproof recipe for how to pick the right colors gives equal weight to one key ingredient that everyone always has at their disposal: **Whatever Makes You Happy!**

Here's the thing: If your personal preferences are at odds with some of the science behind a color, not only is that totally valid but it's also a designer-approved position, through and through. (So if studies show that blue is calming, but you've just never been a fan of blue, you have my full blessing and official stamp of approval to avoid blue at all costs.)

Because that's kind of how colors work: Each one is an infinitely expandable container of meaning. White can stand for purity at an American wedding, but in other cultures, it's the color of death and mourning. And based on your personal experience with the color, white may be positive, neutral, or negative.

Take your time figuring out how you feel about a color.

At the end of the day, picking the "right" colors for a space is kind of a mixed bag. But the important thing is that you take a minute to figure out how you personally feel and respond to colors before forging ahead—especially if the color updates you're looking into aren't easily reversible. (And don't worry: I've got lots of easy, low-commitment tips for how to incorporate color—it doesn't always have to be a full paint job!)

Bottom line: Color's palpable effects on mood are just too good to pass up, and when it comes to your mental wellness, every little bit helps.

Color is endlessly versatile, deeply emotional, and always makes an impact, whether you know it or not.

EVERY COLOR IS A MOOD

UP

DOWN

MOOD

Because these colors are stimulating and energizing, I generally tend to go for these shades when designing more public rooms, like living rooms, kitchens, and dining rooms.

Generally speaking, **warm shades are energy lifting** and **cool colors are energy calming.**

Because these colors are soothing and calming, I tend to go for these shades when designing more private rooms, like bedrooms and bathrooms.

Neutrals Are Non-negotiables

Neutrals will always be in the mix, whether you're opting for a solid, goes-with-everything base color or using them as accents for a bolder, color-driven room. Be careful, though: Too much neutral might feel sterile or institutional, so if you do want to go for a tone-on-tone look, make sure you layer in textures, shapes, and patterns to keep things dimensional, engaging, and interesting.

Technically, every color in this room is considered a neutral. But thanks to textural layers (Leather! Linen! Wool!) and strategic contrasting elements (black tables, curtain rods, and accents), this space is anything but boring.

Setting the Right Tone

The beauty of color is that any shade can be adjusted to feel warmer or cooler, brighter or lighter, deeper or softer.

WARM	NEUTRAL	COOL

PRO TIP

If you love updating your accents and decor throughout the year, opt for more neutral undertones for your foundational pieces (sofas and tables) over anything too warm or cool to minimize color clashing.

porcelain eg

periwinkle fog mi

dusty rose flamin

plum eggplant cla

an saddle rust ter

cantaloupe musta

chartreuse olive

cobalt lapis navy

ru linen oat greige

t ash heather slate

o magenta raisin

et cherry auburn

a-cotta tangerine

rd saffron lemon

sage grass pine

bsidian

WHICH COLOR IS SPEAKING TO YOU?

Believe it or not, this is the tip of the iceberg in terms of how many different hues of a shade exist! Amazing, isn't it? Try not to come in with too many preconceived notions about a color—you may not consider yourself a green person but, in the right shade with the right undertone, you could be pleasantly surprised!

provide you with even a
few seconds of zen while
you're working from home
(blue has been shown
to lower the heart rate),
isn't that more than
worth the full paint job?
(Answer: Hell yes.)

If You're Reading This While Painting, It's Too Late

Paint color is a pain to reverse (and is a decision that affects your mood in a big way), so here's how to make sure you come to an informed decision before you commit.

1. Home is where the more accurate light is.

The fluorescent lights used in stores can distort the way a color looks. From peel + stick swatches to cheaper sample cans you can purchase, there are lots of ways to test colors out before shelling out for multiple paint cans. Pro tip: Test paint on scraps of paper or poster/foam board (use double-sided tape to attach them to your walls). This will save you a round of paint removal when it comes time to paint your walls for real.

2. It hits different (on all four walls).

Keep in mind that paint colors will look markedly different, depending on the direction the wall faces, what color your floors are, what furniture is close to it, the time of day, the type of lightbulbs you be using in the space—even what's outside the window (i.e., plants or trees will give your walls a subtly greenish cast during the day).

3. Get in your feelings.

Give it a minute (or a few days). Really give yourself a chance to figure out how the color makes you feel—especially monitor how your feelings shift when you enter and leave the space.

BONUS TIP

Figure out your flooring first! There are way less flooring choices than there are paint colors, so if you choose your wall color first, you're severely limiting the flooring options that'll complement your walls.

Online (Paint Color) Dating

The Good, Bad, and Utterly Inaccurate

Starting your color exploration online is great—just make sure you don't end it there. Because seeing something on a screen isn't ever going to represent how you experience it IRL. (And neither will seeing it in a book for that matter!) Your monitor distorts undertones and saturation, so when it comes to color, you must see it in person, in the real room, with the real light, with your real furniture. Plan to spend some time with the color before making your decision. In the meantime, give these color profiles a scroll before you decide to swipe (your wall) with a tester swatch.

Red

TONE: Warm

SUMMARY: I'm intense AF. My friends would say I'm kinda polarizing because I stand for both love and anger, Cupid and the Devil, beauty and toxicity (a red rose is harmless but certain red snakes are poison).

WHERE YOU MIGHT'VE SEEN ME: Logos (Netflix, Coca-Cola, Target . . . what can I say, brands love me, I stand out), marking up a test you did poorly on (sorry for the PTSD), somewhere inside the last sale email you deleted probably . . .

I THINK IT'S SO INTERESTING THAT . . . in some cultures, I'm seen as a symbol of good luck, but in others, I'm seen as a bad omen.

SOMETHING YOU SHOULD KNOW ABOUT ME: I can sometimes help you win (some studies have shown that athletes who wear me win more games) and sometimes mess with your head (students who looked at me right before a test performed worse than students who didn't). What can I say? I'm a mixed bag.

NUMBER OF STUDIES BEHIND MY IMPACT IRL: A lot. I'm one of the most studied colors out there. I've been shown to increase your heart rate (it's sometimes exciting, but if you struggle with anxiety, we may not be a good fit), increase your blood pressure, and up your metabolism (restaurants love me because I've been shown to increase your appetite).

YOU SHOULD SWIPE (YOUR WALL WITH A SAMPLE OF ME) IF . . . you like high-energy, high-impact vibes in your space.

GET OUT

Orange

TONE: Warm

SUMMARY: I'm a red-yellow hybrid—a more mellow version of red but deeper than yellow.

WHERE YOU MIGHT'VE SEEN ME: Halloween, Thanksgiving, during an amazing sunset, being bottomless during brunches and on redheads (let's be real, gingers are really orangeheads! Case in point: Lucille Ball in technicolor).

I THINK IT'S SO INTERESTING THAT . . . I can actually trick you into making you think a room feels warmer than it really is!

WHAT I DO TO ENERGY: Bring it up! My friends would generally say I give off friendly, positive vibes.

SOMETHING YOU SHOULD KNOW ABOUT ME: I'm pretty much up for anything! I'm a great life-of-the-party type if red is not totally to your taste.

NUMBER OF STUDIES BEHIND MY IMPACT IRL: Not a ton, TBH. A few studies have shown that I can help improve cognitive function and alertness, but mostly I'm a great, fun contrast to neutral shades. I'm my best self in social spaces like kitchens, living rooms, and dining rooms.

YOU SHOULD SWIPE (YOUR WALL WITH A SAMPLE OF ME) IF . . . you want to add energy or warmth to a space.

Yellow

TONE: Warm

I THINK IT'S SO INTERESTING THAT . . . I can actually get deep, too. Mute the tone and I become Ms. Sophisticated in a flash (hello, modern vibes).

WHAT I DO TO ENERGY: Shoot it through the roof.

WHAT I DO TO GLOOM: Kick it to the curb. Your woke-up-on-the-wrong-side-of-the-bed 'tude is no match for me.

SOMETHING YOU SHOULD KNOW ABOUT ME: I'm actually technically the brightest color in the rainbow! Some fire trucks and emergency vehicles are using me now instead of red because I can be seen from a distance on a dark night (look, Ma, no lights).

NUMBER OF STUDIES BEHIND MY IMPACT IRL: Not a whole lot. The main thing you should keep in mind is that I am quite stimulating, if I do say so myself, so if a calm-down is what you need, I'm NOT the one to call (hey, self-awareness is important).

YOU SHOULD SWIPE (YOUR WALL WITH A SAMPLE OF ME) IF . . . you want to inject a space with a shot of visual espresso.

Green

TONE: Cool

SUMMARY: I'm pretty outdoorsy. I'm always in nature, which is why I give off a soothing energy.

WHERE YOU MIGHT'VE SEEN ME: That epic first scene in *The Sound Of Music* (the hills are alive with *me*), eco-friendly brands, pretty much every tree out there, and St. Patty's Day festivities.

WHAT I DO TO ENERGY: Mellow it out and promote healing vibes

WHAT I STAND FOR: Growth, harmony, balance (the good stuff)

SOMETHING YOU SHOULD KNOW ABOUT ME: By definition, I'm the easiest to see (being in the middle of the rainbow means, wavelength wise, your eyes don't have to strain as hard to see me). It's also why I'm very calming (hospitals and schools love me).

NUMBER OF STUDIES BEHIND MY IMPACT IRL: A decent amount. I've been shown to be restorative and have even been shown to help accelerate recovery in patients with Parkinson's disease.

YOU SHOULD SWIPE (YOUR WALL WITH A SAMPLE OF ME) IF . . . you want a calming effect but aren't a blue person.

Blue

TONE: Cool

SUMMARY: Not to brag, but I'm universally everyone's favorite! I'm chill, easygoing, and I pretty much get along with anyone.

WHAT I DO TO ENERGY: Bring it down in the best possible way (a lot of people say I'm really good at helping them stay calm). Lights tinted with me have been shown to decrease suicide and crime rates so I'm often used at places like bridges and train stations.

SPECIAL SKILLS: I'm the only color that has been shown to suppress appetite because, outside of blueberries, food/nature isn't normally where you'd find me. (If you hate counting calories, investing in blue dinnerware could help you eat less!)

SOMETHING YOU SHOULD KNOW ABOUT ME: I'm a good fit for people with anxiety (so if that's you, let's definitely get together).

NUMBER OF STUDIES BEHIND MY IMPACT IRL: A ton. I've been shown to enhance creativity and productivity (probably because of the calming thing) and lower heart rate, body temperature, and blood pressure.

YOU SHOULD SWIPE (YOUR WALL WITH A SAMPLE OF ME) IF . . . you need help staying calm, have trouble relaxing or keeping stress at bay, and want to maximize productivity in a room.

Purple

TONE: Cool

SUMMARY: I'm really well balanced (a mix of warm red + cool blue) and a bit of a rare occurrence all around.

NICKNAME: Violet

I THINK IT'S SO INTERESTING THAT . . . I've been associated with royalty for quite some time, and that vibe has stuck! My deeper shades may feel pretty formal, reverent, and kinda bougie.

WHAT I DO TO ENERGY: I've been shown to help inspire creativity and get your imagination going!

JUST A HEADS-UP: Sometimes, I'm known to trigger sadness, so make sure to calibrate my tone before you decide to commit.

MY FAVORITE PLACES TO HANG: WFH spaces are my jam. Also, if you mix me with gray, I become this cool, soothing shade—great for bathrooms and bedrooms.

YOU SHOULD SWIPE (YOUR WALL WITH A SAMPLE OF ME) IF . . . you are in the mood for something a little unconventional or interesting.

color is

VISCERAL

EMOTIONAL

MEDICINAL

POWERFUL

FOR EVERYONE

COLOR COMMITMENTS

There are so many ways to experiment with color that don't have to involve a full-on paint job. Starting with accessories that you can change out seasonally is a great way to dip your toes in before investing in more permanent design choices.

➤ **IT'S CASUAL.**

Accessories you can easily switch out (blankets, pillows) are the perfect, low-commitment way to try out a new color.

➤ **IT'S A [CHANGEABLE] COMMITMENT.**

Scared of paint or wallpaper? Enter accent walls. If you're not feeling it, you have to remove it from only one wall (and not four).

➤ IT'S EXCLUSIVE (KINDA).

My favorite reversible design decision
is, without a doubt, peel-and-stick
wallpaper. Don't love it? Peel it right off
with no damage to your walls.

COLOR PALETTE QUICKIE #183: Pull out your favorite shades from a work of art or painting.

Okay, but How Do I Get Started?

You can quite literally start anywhere.

HAPPINESS TIP #473: Pull out textures and colors from a favorite photo. (Bonus: Colors that remind you of a fun or memorable time are also an instant shot of serotonin.)

(Color) Tricks Are for Everyone

Using Color to Make the Most of Any Space

Check out some of my favorite ways to use color strategically to maximize how spaces are seen and experienced.

▲ TEMPERATURE CHECK

Some colors actually affect the perception of how cold or warm you feel. For chillier spaces, it might help to bring in warmer shades for the walls or decor.

▲ SIZE MATTERS ➤

When a space feels tight, it can make you feel trapped and even depressed. Going for lighter colors makes any space feel airier and wider.

I love the process of finding just the right balance with color—if the overall palette is minimal, I pump up the texture and pattern. If I'm bringing in a wider range of shades, I tone down the other elements (shapes, prints) to temper the energy.

Calmergizing

[kahm-er-jahz-ing]

adjective

The inexplicably amazing feeling of walking into a well-balanced, beautifully designed space, i.e., when the design is soothing but not snoozy, interesting but not over-the-top, fully functional and fully gorgeous at the same time

Color Quickies

Not all color decisions have to involve a time-consuming process that has to lead to a forever choice. Sometimes you just need to see if you can catch a vibe before you commit. I totally get it. So here's a speed round for ya: the old Accessories Switcheroo.

1

BLACK AND WHITE FEEL CLEAN, CRISP, AND MODERN.

2

DEEP ORANGE WARMS UP THE SPACE.

3

THE RUG? SO FUN.
LET IT LEAD THE WAY.

(COLOR) PALETTE
Cleansers

Calming Palettes

Remember: You register color in your subconscious, your nervous system. Cool colors have been proven to lower heart rate and blood pressure, so try some of these soothing color combos to help bring things down a notch (great for anyone who struggles with anxiety and feelings of being overwhelmed).

Zen AF

Say Ahhhhhh

Out of Office

Energizing Palettes

Liven up more "public" rooms (living rooms, dining rooms, family rooms)—or any room than could use an extra pick-me-up (a bleh guest bathroom, a kid's space, a bonus room). I also go for these palettes when designing for anyone who struggles with low mood and energy levels.

Party time

Morning Sunrise

Ready for anything

My Foolproof Faves

Check out my go-to paint colors in every shade.

Gray Areas

My neutral standbys help balance out the brights.

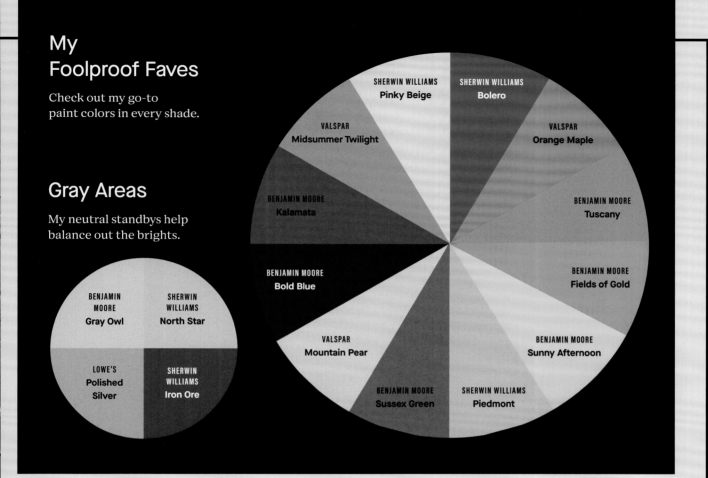

SHERWIN WILLIAMS
Pinky Beige

SHERWIN WILLIAMS
Bolero

VALSPAR
Midsummer Twilight

VALSPAR
Orange Maple

BENJAMIN MOORE
Kalamata

BENJAMIN MOORE
Tuscany

BENJAMIN MOORE
Bold Blue

BENJAMIN MOORE
Fields of Gold

VALSPAR
Mountain Pear

BENJAMIN MOORE
Sunny Afternoon

BENJAMIN MOORE
Sussex Green

SHERWIN WILLIAMS
Piedmont

BENJAMIN MOORE
Gray Owl

SHERWIN WILLIAMS
North Star

LOWE'S
Polished Silver

SHERWIN WILLIAMS
Iron Ore

Creative Palettes

Hit that creative sweet spot with a mix that's not overstimulating but also not too chill (you need *some* juice to get those ideas going!). Try these palettes in a home office, a kid's playroom, or any public/group space.

Ready, set, ideate

Manifestation Station

Visual Caffeine

Chapter 5
The Good Bits

———————————————

Color has a powerful effect on mood.

———————————————

Warm colors pump you up (and are great for rooms
where you need to entertain and gather); cool colors
chill you out (and work best in private rooms,
like bedrooms and bathrooms).

———————————————

You can make any color work in any space
by adjusting the tone.

———————————————

Explore color by testing it out in smaller doses.

———————————————

THE

Work-from-Home

INSTRUCTION MANUAL

Love it or hate it, the work-from-home space is probably here to stay, at least in some form. The key is to figure out how to maximize productivity, keep stress levels at bay during the workday, and draw healthy boundaries with it all when you clock out for the night.

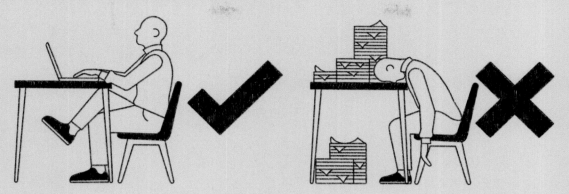

Of course, this needs to be attacked from both ends. Make sure you're taking care of yourself, getting your needs met, and doing your best to stay mentally healthy. Because here's the paradox: Not being productive is both a symptom of—and cause for—mental unwellness. It's a vicious cycle really: If you're not well, you're less productive. And when you're less productive, you feel awful.

Thoughtful workspace design can help eliminate distractions when you do hunker down to get some work done. And while I can't wrestle your phone away from you, I can advise you on tips to help optimize your space to work harder for you so that from the moment you sit down, you're actually excited to get to work (legitimately!), and focusing on the task at hand is literally the only thing you feel like doing.

(DESIGN) TOOLS* YOU'LL NEED

(*Make sure you have all tools before starting assembly.)

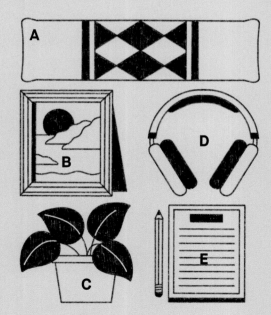

A: Comfort

B: Inspiration

C: Destressors

D: Separation

E: Organization

F: The knowledge that overworking is not noble, admirable, or an attribute that adds more worth or value to you as a human being.

BOBBERNOMICS 101

Workplace design that's easy on your pain points and your eyes

After social media, there's nothing more distracting than pain. Whether it's sore wrists, chronic back issues, or stiff shoulders, pain takes up a lot of mental space. Imagine freeing up that space for what you actually need to focus on—and how much more productive you'll be as a result. But a painless setup should also be painless to look at every day—which is incidentally my M.O. when it comes to workplace design.

 YAY
De-stressors

 NAY
Comfort

___

PRO TIP: Use a laptop stand to prevent neck strain.

 NAY
Comfort

___

PRO TIP: Add cushions to support longer periods of sitting.

 YAY
Organization

THE PRODUCTIVITY PARADOX

Work smarter by *not* working (yes, you read that right).

TAKE A BREAK.

MOVE YOUR BODY.

EAT SOMETHING.

DO SOMETHING ELSE.

Tons of studies show that taking real, genuine breaks actually improves your performance. That's because the brain naturally works in "bursts" of high and low activity. (So forcing yourself to work through a lower energy period could prove to be counterproductive.) Try to disconnect even for five minutes to do something totally unrelated, then come back to your work.

I love designing spots that allow for this—whether it's a comfy chair in the corner or a cluster of plants nearby to encourage someone to water them during breaks. Anything that involves stepping away from your desk and disengaging from your work is going to help you do your work better when you get back to your desk.

3

DRAW BOUNDARIES

For anyone working from home, the most important boundary to be mindful of is the line between work and play (and by play, I mean everything in life that's NOT work!). When this line gets blurry, you're setting yourself up for a massive, mess of a work/life balance. Not ever being able to turn off will wreak havoc on your mental health.

While setting up a workspace in a separate room is ideal, not all of us have the space to do that. There are tons of ways to tuck in a spot to work in any room of the house. Integrating the style into the rest of the room will help it feel cohesive/connected to the rest of the larger space, but remember to create mental distance by shutting down for the night,

even if it's as simple as closing your laptop when you're done for the day (or better yet, stashing it away in a drawer so you don't see it). In the end, a work-from-home space is sort of a delicate balancing act between making sure the space feels intentional and designated and adopting an "out of sight, out of mind" approach.

ORG CHART

Some of us need more stuff accessible to us during the workday than others. It all depends on what you do and how you do it. My general rule of thumb is to keep most things contained/out of sight for a more streamlined, focus-friendly (and mind-calming) setup. But if you do need some stuff to be easily reachable throughout the day, make sure you invest in quality pieces and prioritize organization that's uniform and quickly recognizable so it's that much easier on the eyes (and, most important, your mind). Noticing a theme here? Yep, oversimplifying everything is the key to freeing up your mind space for focused, productive work. TBH, workspace design really boils down to removing excuses! The goal is to make sure every time you're in this space, there's literally nothing left to do but . . . get to work.

Love this closet-nook-turned-WFH space.

PRO TIP: I'd add a room divider or put up a curtain to fully section this off for when you're ready to call it a night.

super easy to reach! ←

WERK FROM HOME

The I-Can't-Wait-to-Get-Shit-Done-in-Here Room

When you're working, you want to be firing on all cylinders. And since your performance is directly impacted by the state of your wellness, work space design that gives your wellness a boost is a must.

This means staying inspired, motivated, and driven while you're in work mode (even if the finish line is as simple as wrapping up emails early so you can start cooking your favorite meal for dinner) is incredibly important and vital for maintaining a work life that brings you some measure of fulfillment. Because the reality is that not all of us are in positions where what we do for a living brings us deep joy. But what we all need every day, no matter where you're at in your life and/or career, are reminders of why we do what we do. Maybe you're at a less-than-ideal job to put your kids through college. Maybe you're part-timing to give yourself flexibility for a small business you're hoping to start soon. Or maybe you're juggling a few smaller roles to eke out rent for your own place because you value your independence. Whatever the case may be, doing what we can to keep our eyes on the prize—whatever that prize is for you—cannot be underestimated. Your day-to-day happiness incrementally adds up to create your overall quality of life and, wherever design can step in to help, I believe that it should.

6

Light Is Everything (Seriously)

It all starts with light.

One of the first things I do when I start designing a space is assess and monitor how much natural light the space gets. Identifying where, when, and how light shines into a room is crucial because light is pretty much pure magic—it can make a cramped space feel bigger, colors appear brighter, and gloomy vibes feel, well, less gloomy. Sounds hokey, right?

Actually, it's not.

Turns out, a "sunny disposition" is called that for a reason—lots of studies support sunlight's connection to a happier, healthier mental state. From mood and energy levels to productivity and sleep quality (yep, sunlight and sleep go hand in hand), light's powerful impact on our (mental) wellness is pretty much a given at this point. It's not a coincidence that when you walk into a bright, light-filled space, you feel inexplicably calmer, more at ease, and, honestly, happier.

And **the best thing about light? It's free.** Even a quick rearranging of your existing pieces can seriously transform a space (and the "afters" will be stunning, I promise!).

In a pinch, artificial light (which includes any source of indoor light, from light bulbs to candles) can do the trick, too.

I'm breaking it all down. But first, let's establish why **light is a nonnegotiable when it comes to your health.**

231

Sunlight Should Be Required Viewing

Natural Light Does More Than Just Look Good

1. I'm a fan of eating outside when you can. Being in the fresh air helps you stay present and mindful while you eat (another mental wellness go-to!); it also exposes you to nature's #1 pick-me-up: sunlight. Because it naturally triggers the release of serotonin (your "happy hormone"), natural light is pretty much a mental wellness MVP in my book.

2. Sunlight exposure first thing in the morning helps activate your appetite hormones, keeping your hunger cues regular throughout the day (which, in turn, helps you regulate your mood. Getting "hangry" is real! Mood, hunger, and mental stability go hand in hand).

3. Breakfast nooks set up near or around a window that gets decent light are a great way to use home design to maximize your health.

PRO TIP

Even sunlight from a cloudy day or a shady spot outside is significantly brighter than the sunniest spot inside your house. So get outside if and when you can!

3

JUMP AHEAD ➤

The sun also helps keep your sleep cycle regular. (Read: You'll get sleepy more naturally at night if you get good sun during the day.) For more on how to use design to maximize sleep, check out my bedroom room guide on page 250.

Light for All

How to Maximize Natural
Light in Any Space

1. Locate It

Take some time to figure out when and where natural light enters your home. Is there a darker area that gets super sunny in the afternoon? (Hello, midday reading nook.) Or a great corner that catches daylight in the AM but gets shadowy after lunch? (Prime real estate for a morning meditation spot, if you ask me.) Light changes at different points during the day, so remember to account for that as you're identifying all the sun-loving spots in your home.

OPPOSITE: The light from this side of the house was too good to pass up, so we opted for glass paneling on the door and shadeless windows up top to maximize it during the day.

ABOVE: Leggy chairs take up less visual weight and maximize *all* the gorgeous light in this room.

2. Work Around It

Figure out how to work with what you've got. Make sure you're not blocking the light you do get (like positioning a bulky couch against a window, for example).

3. Reflect It

You can't talk about how to maximize light without talking about surfaces (walls, tables, and countertops). From material types to colors and finishes—all of these things affect how light bounces around in a space. You don't have to plan on a full-on paint job, though you can if you're game (I'm a big fan of a solid paint refresh). Things like sticking to a neutral/light color palette, choosing glossy over matte finishes, and strategically placing mirrors can all work in your favor—you'll feel like you're in a wider, airier, light-filled room in no time.

Multiple mirrors and a glossy, bright white countertop help bounce light all over the place.

No Windows?
No Problem.

When natural light is at a premium, it's worth thinking as out-of-the-box as you can with it. (Light is too important for your health not to.) This windowless bathroom felt cramped and dark, so I added warm Edison bulbs up top and a fun neon fixture for a cozy glow all around. The mirror helps reflect and bounce all this light around the room.

It's Okay to Have (Light) Control Issues

Customizing the Light You Have

As amazing as natural light is for your health, it's important to be able to block out most of it at night. Too much light exposure toward the end of the day hinders your body's natural melatonin production (the hormone that triggers sleepiness at night). There's nothing more frustrating—or worse for your health, both mental and physical—than not being able to sleep when you need to.

There's also the issue of privacy, which all of us need in varying degrees to feel protected and safe in our homes. All in all, design that helps you maximize natural light during the day and minimize it at night when you're winding down is crucial for your health.

Hello, sunshine!

OPPOSITE: For full coverage in rooms where needing to sleep through the night is paramount, pair blackout curtains with blackout shades.

No shade? All good.

If your space is already light-challenged and/or limited in terms of the natural light it gets, opt for no shades at all. In fact, remove existing shades altogether if you feel comfortable doing so.

OPPOSITE: Complete privacy without sacrificing gorgeous natural light = the best of both worlds.

Blackout Shades Don't Have to Be Black

Nowadays, shades come in many different colors and styles. I love being able to customize the look of a room without sacrificing desired coverage level.

Light-Bulb Moments

Indoor Lighting Dos + Don'ts

When sunlight is hard to come by (especially if you're in a part of the world that doesn't get a ton of sunlight regularly), a bright white light bulb will definitely help get your system up and running during the day. LEDs have become the gold standard (you can even find them in vintage styles, like Edisons!) and for good reason: They're super energy-efficient, 100 percent nontoxic, and come in all different light temperatures and intensities so you can easily customize your look.

BLUE LIGHT ISN'T ALL BAD

Blue-light wavelengths—found in the sun (which is partly why the sun is so bright)—are actually something you need during the day. Without any blue light at all, you won't feel energized. That's why it's key that you monitor blue-light exposure without blocking it altogether. Since it suppresses melatonin—the hormone that makes you feel sleepy—just avoid it at night and you're good to go.

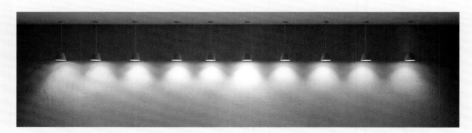

GO WARMER/SOFTER FOR LIGHTS YOU USE AT NIGHT.   ←——————→   **GO BRIGHTER/ COOLER DURING THE DAY.**

Many Lights Are Better Than One

Indoor lighting in the home should be set up to support all the needs of any given room so that it can function optimally. When a space isn't properly set up to function well, you're putting extra strain on the users of the room, incurring an emotional cost (frustration, annoyance) that will add up (oh, trust me, it will—whether you think you "feel" it or not).

When it comes to indoor lighting specifically, I focus on three major layers to ensure an optimally functioning space:

1. AMBIENT
Evenly distributed, diffused light. Natural light from a window or an overhead light like a pendant, chandelier, or recessed lighting are all fair game.

2. ACCENT
Decorative lights that draw attention to a focal point like artwork or architectural details. Strategically backlighting spots like alcoves, behind furniture pieces, or steps on a staircase creates a dramatic effect (think mood lighting).

3. TASK
Usually brighter than ambient lighting. Task lights are directional and used for specific activities like reading, working, or cooking.

BRIGHT LIGHTS, HAPPY KITCHEN

Recessed lighting and natural light from the window give this kitchen plenty of ambient light while the pendant and under-cabinet lights provide great directional lighting (for cooking, chopping, and eating). BONUS: The under-cabinet lights double as accent lighting—perfect for setting the mood on a low-key night in.

THE LIGHTING CHART

To cover all your bases, ambient and task are the two most important types of lighting to incorporate in your design. Depending on the type of light bulbs you use, task lighting can do double duty as evening lighting, as it tends to be less bright (good for bedside lamps). Directional/accent lighting may be optional and is usually more of a style choice than anything else. Candles fall under this category, which can definitely help with the evening wind-down, when you shouldn't be using bright lights anyway.

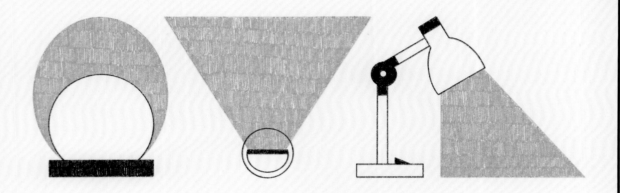

1. AMBIENT

→ RECESSED

→ CEILING LIGHTS
  (CHANDELIERS,
  PENDANTS)

→ SCONCES

→ TRACK LIGHTS

→ FLOOR LAMPS

→ NATURAL LIGHT

2. ACCENT

→ RECESSED

→ CANDLES

→ SCONCES

→ HIDDEN FIXTURES

3. TASK

→ DESK + TABLE LAMPS

→ SCONCES

→ SMALL PENDANTS

→ UNDER-CABINET LIGHTING

The natural light in the middle of this stairway was too good to pass up, so I set up a simple dining area (an extra spot to eat and gather is never a bad idea).

Chapter 6
The Good Bits

Designing around light is crucial,
both for good design and good health.

Regular sunlight during the day helps regulate your
energy levels, metabolism, and mood—and even
helps you sleep better at night.

Maximize light during the day, minimize light at night.

Support the various functions of a space by incorporating
different types of lighting throughout the room.

THE
10 Bedroom
Mantras
TO LIVE BY

(and Fall Asleep To)

1 I will honor my body and mind by making sleep a nonnegotiable priority.

2 Sleep is not a reward I need to "earn"—it's an absolute necessity for my mental and physical health.

3 Designing my bedroom to help me sleep better isn't frivolous—it's an important, health-improving activity.

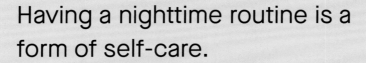

Having a nighttime routine is a form of self-care.

Okay, so let's be real. Smartphones kind of own us now, making "turning off" pretty much impossible. But the act of carving out time to prepare for sleep—a crucial, restorative activity for your mind and body—is key (and the operative phrase here is "prepare for"). Here's why: When it comes to habits, your neurons are wired to love repetition, so when it comes to building a nightly routine, the way you plan out your wind-down process will, in time, become super automatic.

Whether it's dimming the lights, lighting a candle, or setting out your pajamas on your bed— whatever that step 1 is for you, start to build an association and be consistent. Soon, you'll notice your mind and body will begin to "rewire" itself. Your nightly wind-down will become as Pavlovian as brushing your teeth at night.

I will accept the facts about sleep.

More and more research is uncovering how insanely vital sleep is for your mental and physical health. Not getting at least seven to eight hours a night messes with your hormone levels, affecting everything from appetite to mood to memory. In fact, there was a study done that showed improving your sleep patterns had more of a measurable, positive effect on people diagnosed with depression than some antidepressants did! (Yep, that's how powerful sleep is.) Good sleep also starts way before you get into bed. Here's a cheat sheet I like to use for eliminating things that might disrupt my sleep:

HOURS BEFORE BED	6	4	3	2	1.5

CUT OFF

CAFFEINE · ALCOHOL · LARGE MEALS · NICOTINE · STRENUOUS EXERCISE

I will calibrate my light intake.

 DAY

In addition to getting regular sunlight, some studies show that watching the sun rise IRL is a healthy way to get your vitamin D. The mix of reddish light waves (infrared) with the blue light (the good kind!) is fantastic for your health, including your mood.

 NIGHT

Chill out your lights at night. Bright light in the evenings (including blue light) can prevent the natural release of melatonin (the hormone that starts up your body's natural sleep program). Incandescents, warmer temp LEDs, and even candles are all fair game.

253

7 I will keep my cool.

Your body temperature naturally lowers before and during sleep to conserve energy, so it's important to keep your bedroom cooler during the night to help facilitate this (65 degrees Fahrenheit is the sweet spot). Higher core body temperatures not only increase the chances of you waking up in the middle of the night but also have been linked to less restorative, slow wave/REM sleep overall. Luckily, there are lots of ways to help cue your body temperature to start cooling off.

COOL YOUR BODY

- Take a lukewarm shower.
- Drink cold water.
- Wear breathable pajamas.

I keep a carafe beside my bed.

COOL THE BED

- Choose breathable fabrics
- Skip the flat sheet.
- Choose a bed frame lower to the ground.

I never use one!

COOL THE ROOM

- Use insulated curtains/window treatments.
- Create airflow using a fan or an open window.
- Turn off all devices (electronics that are plugged in produce heat).

Cotton, hemp, and linen are some of my faves — for bedding and pajamas

I will declutter my nightstand.

When it comes to the bedroom, my advice is to always keep things as simple as possible. You want to be cognizant of what's in your line of sight, especially in a room that should be tailored to help you shut down. Now, that's not to say your bedroom should be boring or plain (remember, your design style is whatever makes you happy!), but there are ways of styling this very personal space that keep your personality intact while optimizing for a good night's sleep. The nightstand in particular is a bedroom workhorse that is prone to becoming a major clutter magnet—it's just way too easy to start piling stuff onto it, so make sure to lean toward keeping it minimal, tidy, and clutter-free.

THE 10 BEDROOM MANTRAS TO LIVE BY (AND FALL ASLEEP TO)

9

I will be intentional about the colors I use in my bedroom.

While I have my personal favorite bedroom colors based on color psychology (remember how strongly I felt about those blue curtains in my childhood bedroom!), I totally get that color is a really personal thing. For example, even though red isn't my first recommendation because it's prone to increase your heart rate (something you DON'T want when you're trying to sleep), I've found ways of toning it down to promote ultimate relaxation (see page 206).

Dusty pink? Soothing. Graphic lines? Bold. Put 'em together and you've got a well-balanced bedroom that's anything but boring.

THE 10 BEDROOM MANTRAS TO LIVE BY (AND FALL ASLEEP TO)

10

I will invest in extra details if I know I struggle with sleep.

If you're not naturally a good sleeper or go through phases where it's tougher than normal, it's worth looking into a few extras to give you an assist.

ANALOG ALARM

Avoid LED lights by the bed with a classic clock (just make sure it's dead silent).

EXTRA SEATING

Don't stay in bed if you struggle with insomnia. It's important to keep the sleep/bed association sacred so that you associate being in bed only with sleeping. If more than twenty minutes go by while you're awake, get out of bed, sit in another area, and do something else relaxing (read, meditate) until you get sleepy again.

AROMA-THERAPY

Eucalyptus and lavender have been shown to help calm the nervous system.

WEIGHTED TEXTILES

Studies have shown that the extra pressure helps lower your heart rate and slow down breathing when you're anxious.

7

Plant-Based Advice

Plants Are Seriously Magic

Plants Are Nature Lite.

Okay, so looking at a potted fern on your desk isn't exactly the same as traipsing through a jungle featured in a Nat Geo documentary or forest bathing in the woodlands of rural Japan (yes, that's a thing!), but it's still scientifically proven to produce major results when it comes to your mental and physical health. Translation? Eat your veggies, do some cardio, and water your plants.

When it comes to design, plants are the whole dang package—not only do they instantly bring life, color, and interest to a space, but they also help soften and balance harder surfaces in spaces like bathrooms and kitchens. (Fact: Design is innately about achieving balance in some way, shape, or form.) Add to that the amazing health benefits (cleaner air! less stress!) and you've got an element I pretty much never do without.

Part of what scientists are uncovering in their research into plants and their massive wellness benefits is the why behind the wow. Studies have shown that the feeling of awe—something you commonly experience when you're immersed in nature—is associated with lower health risks for lots of conditions, like heart disease, depression, and type 2 diabetes. Studies also show that the feeling of being connected to nature is closely tied to the deeper feeling of having a meaningful purpose in the world (which is a key component of happiness). Yep, even a walk in the park during your lunch break can trigger some of these benefits!

Since most of us probably aren't in a position to schedule a luxurious, uninterrupted nature sesh on a regular basis (according to studies, the amount of exposure time needed to experience the benefits of nature is about two full hours), having plants around is the next-best thing.

Studies show that even looking at images of nature can provide the same benefits (though not to the same degree). But, hey, we take what we can get, right?

What *Don't* Plants Do?

➤ They calm you down

SLOW THE HEART RATE

SUPPRESS THE NERVOUS SYSTEM

LOWER BLOOD PRESSURE

LOWER STRESS HORMONE LEVELS

➤ They make you feel less lonely

CONNECT YOU WITH NATURE

GIVE YOU A SENSE OF PURPOSE

➤ They boost your mood

SOIL RELEASES A CHEMICAL THAT TRIGGERS SEROTONIN (YOUR HAPPY HORMONE)

DECREASE SYMPTOMS OF ANXIETY AND DEPRESSION

➤ They make you healthier

IMPROVE IMMUNE SYSTEM FUNCTION

CLEAN THE AIR BY REMOVING AIRBORNE POLLUTANTS, TOXINS, AND EVEN MOLD

➤ They increase your productivity

IMPROVE COGNITIVE FUNCTION AND PERFORMANCE

IMPROVE MEMORY RETENTION

IMPROVE FOCUS AND CONCENTRATION

ABOVE: I love how this reddish rubber plant, while echoing the warm tones in this kids' space, is also a fun focal point.

OPPOSITE: Plants can also add drama (the good kind). This dark green, variegated rubber tree adds a subtle color accent—and a bit of life—to this black-white-metallic color scheme.

Plant Styling 101

The trick with plants is to treat them as you would any other decor piece or accessory. Think about shape, color, vibe, and how the plant looks within the context of the rest of the space.

mix up the styles →

LESS IS MORE ➜

If you're nervous about plant parenting, even a few is better than none. For all my best tips on how to care for your plants, jump to page 286.

mix up the height

go BIG with just one iconic plant

Everybody Puts Baby In the Corner

Boring, empty spot, you've met your match. Give it up for my favorite hero houseplants (aka the no-brainer way to do plants).

LEFT: Fiddleleaf figs are pretty much foolproof.

ABOVE: Spiky and tall yucca, meet low and curved chair. (Hello, gorgeous contrast.)

OPPOSITE: Meet the banana leaf plant (aka the seriously-looks-good-anywhere plant).

FACT: Shallow pots make for deeper conversations (because shorter plants won't block your view across the table).

POT HACK #541: Spray-paint a boring pot to match your decor.

Pot Lovers
Welcome

From oversize cups to baskets to pots of all shapes, sizes, and styles—whatever you choose to contain your plants is another way to make a style statement and add texture to your space.

Branch Out

Branches are kind of like the low-maintenance version of plants (look, Ma, no soil). They add drama, interest, and sculptural contrast to a modern space. Just add water and you're good to go.

PRO TIP

Make sure your vase is strong enough to hold the weight—branches, especially taller ones, can often be heavy and unruly.

Nature-First Design

In addition to getting plant-happy, prioritizing nature in home design can happen in a lot of different ways. From being mindful of what the view outside your window (even if it's as "normal" as a small grassy knoll in your neighborhood) to exploring gardening as a mental wellness activity (if you have the space for it!)—both of these can give you the same benefits. Literally just *being* anywhere green does the trick. Studies show that even viewing images of nature can help lower stress levels (though getting outside and experiencing the real deal will always produce better results).

OPPOSITE: I love how this leafy wallpaper evokes a real jungle. Since it's been applied end to end and across the ceiling, it makes walking through this hallway an immersive, nature-inspired experience.

RIGHT: Get imaginative. This sweet indoor swing's faux vines are a lovely take on nature-inspired design for kids (plus, check out all the green they'll see through the window outside).

Design that Connects You to Nature

Part of what studies continue to confirm is the powerful idea that we as humans are inherently part of, deeply connected to, and sustained by nature. The more we are reminded of this, the better, calmer, happier, and more purposeful we feel. Biophilic design stems from this idea of being part of a larger whole—it's the practice of incorporating naturally occurring elements (materials, shapes, ideas) into built design. This can range from something as simple as a table crafted from solid wood to a chair silhouette inspired by the golden ratio to an outdoor/indoor space that blurs the boundaries between outside and in.

RIGHT: All-wood everything. The many types of wood-grain textures present on this outdoor table-scape bring to mind all the different types of trees used to make everyday items.

OPPOSITE: A treehouse, but make it chic. Keeping this window uncovered during a work sesh makes you feel fully immersed in nature, as do all the various wood surfaces layered inside.

Chapter 7
The Good Bits

Plants are insanely good for your mental and physical health. If being in nature regularly isn't an option for you, plants are actually a closer second than you might think.

Style plants like you would anything else in your home—think about shape, color, and contrast.

Try incorporating nature in other ways, too (it'll have the same effects)—frame photos of it, make sure you can see it out your window, bring the outside in (branches are your friend).

Raising Good ~~Kids~~

Plants

A FIELD GUIDE FOR
FIRST-TIME PLANT PARENTS

Let's skip the "Congratulations on your new bundle of joy" part and cut to the chase: Plants are snowflakes.

Did you know that even two snake plants might require different care tactics? (Yeah, like I said. Snowflakes.) Even plants that are labeled "low maintenance" often turn out to be, well, not that low maintenance (hello, withering succulents). That's because each plant is, in fact, a unique living thing. And TBH, some plants are just born with better genes.

It's important to know the basics (sun, water, overall room temp) but also equally vital to know that each plant will respond differently to things, so the best rule of thumb is to adjust as you go along. Check in on your little guys. (Part of the mood boost you get is from the act of nurturing another living thing, so lean into it, you caregiver you.)

It's totally normal to have some feels here. (Dread? Stress? PTSD from the last dead plant you had to toss?) But the mood and wellness benefits are just too good to pass up, so along with how to think about your rooms when it comes to plants, I've also included some of my best tips for how to keep our green friends healthy, happy and thriving.

From prepping your tool kit to troubleshooting common plant problems to understanding climate control—we're leaving no stone unturned.

THE NEW PLANT PARENT
Starter Pack

It can be overwhelming trying to figure out what you need to keep your plants alive and well. Here's my go-to list of must-haves for starting out as a new plant parent. As you get more plant savvy, you'll probably start to phase out some of these tools, and that's totally okay.

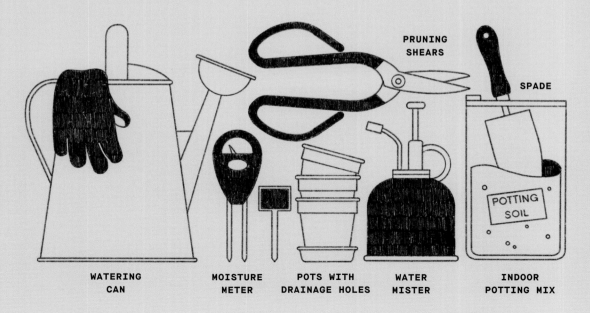

PRUNING SHEARS

SPADE

POTTING SOIL

WATERING CAN   MOISTURE METER   POTS WITH DRAINAGE HOLES   WATER MISTER   INDOOR POTTING MIX

THESE
BABIES NEED
Light

Nothing is more of a bummer for plants than being brought home to a room that doesn't provide the kind of light they need to grow and thrive. Contrary to popular belief, most homes are considered a low-light environment. (Even if you have wall-to-wall windows, depending on what direction your house faces, you could still be blocking out most of the sun's direct beams.) Scope out the light sitch before deciding where to home your new bundles of joy. You can always move things around and see how your plant responds—they'll "tell" you whether they're happy where you've put them.

NONE	LOW LIGHT	INDIRECT
A windowless room (like an office or small bathroom)—believe it or not, there are plants that can survive under these conditions!	If you can't read without turning on a lamp, it's a low-light space. Typically it's seven feet or more from the nearest window. **FIG. 1**	Steady, mid-level filtered or obstructed light at about the halfway point between the window and back wall **FIG. 2**

FACT: Light from being in the shade is considered indirect sunlight; there are plants out there that can grow in full shade conditions!

1. LOW LIGHT

2. INDIRECT LIGHT

Your plants will tell you if they're happy.

INDIRECT-BRIGHT

Masquerades as direct light but is really just light that's steady and fairly bright throughout the day (often from a sunny window that might even get a bit of direct sunlight for an hour or so)

FIG. 3

DIRECT-INDOORS

Bright sunbeams that directly hit the plant through a window (if you'd need to wear sunblock while spending time near a window that's in direct sunlight)

FIG. 4

DIRECT-OUTDOORS

Direct, outdoor sun exposure will always be significantly more intense than even the sunniest window so be careful when placing indoor plants outside, even for a short while, as they could burn.

3. INDIRECT-BRIGHT LIGHT

4. DIRECT LIGHT

NORTH-FACING WINDOWS
generally have lower light conditions/
minimal direct sunlight so make sure
the plants you home here are used to
those conditions.

MOST INTENSE: N/A
(at most, you'll get gentle,
diffused light)

EAST-FACING WINDOWS
are where you see the sun rise.
Morning light is technically direct light,
but it tends to be softer, so plants that
love indirect light can still tolerate it.

MOST INTENSE: The AM
(direct but soft)

WEST-FACING WINDOWS
are where you see the sun set. As the
day progresses, the sunlight gets
more and more intense, so monitor
which plants are receiving that late-in-
the-day sun.

MOST INTENSE: Afternoon (direct)

SOUTH-FACING WINDOWS
get the most daylight! You'll get a mix of
direct and bright indirect light. Farther
away from the window, you'll get solid
indirect light as well.

MOST INTENSE: Late morning to
midafternoon (direct)

What to Do
WHEN THE BABY CRIES

Okay, so they're not going to cry, but they will "tell" you when
something's wrong. Here's a quick lesson in plant-speak.

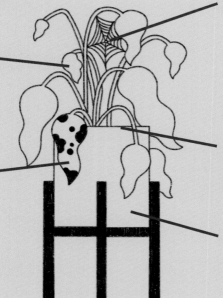

I'M BUGGING OUT
Movement deters bugs (fact: spiderwebs
need stillness to exist). Natural air
currents allow plants in the wild to move
regularly, so to mimic this, adjust your
plant placement and wipe dust off the
leaves to give them a nudge from time
to time.

I NEED SUN
A slower growth rate (wilting,
fewer new leaves sprouting)
means you should try moving your
plant to a sunnier spot for at least
parts of the day.

I'M THIRSTY
Stick your finger in the soil—it should
feel moist and damp. If it's dry and
crumbly, your baby needs water, stat.

I NEED A HAIRCUT
Leaf and leaf parts with abnormal
discoloration should be removed
so your plant can (re)direct
nutrients to its healthy leaves.

I NEED A NEW HOUSE
If the root-to-soil ratio is
becoming unruly (do you see
more roots than soil when you pull
your plant out?), it's time to repot.

MAKE YOUR PLANTS FEEL
Right at Home

In the same way that a lot of babies do well in environments that mimic the womb, it's your job as a plant parent to mimic the plant's native environment as much as possible. Remember—plants are legit pieces of nature IRL that were born in a wild environment. Living in your home is technically a disruption for them. Though you can't perfectly replicate the plant's natural habitat, you can come close (and try to adjust for the discrepancies).

MOIST + HUMID

- LUSH, WARM + WET

- HEAVY RAINFALL (WITH A BRIEF DRY SEASON)

- 70 TO 85 DEGREES FAHRENHEIT

DRY + SUNNY

- DRY HEAT WITH TEMPS PEAKING IN SUMMER

- VERY LIMITED PRECIPITATION (WITH HIGH EVAPORATION)

DARK + WARM

- DARKER; SUNLIGHT IS LOW, DAPPLED, OR SCATTERED.

- SOIL WILL STILL BE MOIST.

- FAIRLY HUMID/WARM

THE *Cheat Sheet*

Check out my go-tos for all you first-timers.

Perfect for bookshelves!

PHILODENDRON

POTHOS

STAGHORN FERN

BEGONIA

PEPEROMIA

ALOE

super low maintenance

MONSTERA

FIDDLELEAF

SNAKE PLANT

Where I Love to Shop

Here is my hit list of sources I turn to for furniture, accessories, lighting, and more that I'm always recommending to friends, family, and clients.

VINTAGE STORES

Chairish / chairish.com / @chairishco

eBay / ebay.com / @ebay

Etsy / etsy.com / @etsy

Everything But the House / ebth.com / @ebth

Facebook Marketplace / facebook.com/marketplace / @facebookmarketplace

Mid Century Møbler / midcenturymobler.com / @midcenturymobler

Noihsaf Bazaar / noihsafbazaar .com/home / @noihsaf.home

Sunbeam Vintage / sunbeamvintage.com / @sunbeam_vintage

FAVORITE LOCAL STORES

Chicago

Anecdote / shopanecdote.com / @shopanecdote

Humboldt House / humboldthouseco.com / @humboldthouse

Jayson Home / jaysonhome.com / @jaysonhome

Los Angeles

Clad Home / cladhome.com / @cladhome

DeKor / dekorliving.com / @dekor.living

Goodies / goodies.la / @goodies.la

Pop Up Home / popuphome.com / @popuphome

New York City

ABC Carpet & Home / abchome .com / @abccarpetandhome

Beam / beambk.com / @beambrooklyn

Fishs Eddy / fishseddy.myshopify.com / @fishseddynyc

Leif / leifshop.com / @leifshop

RETAIL STORES

AllModern / allmodern.com / @allmodern

Annie Selke / annieselke.com / @annieselke

Anthropologie / anthropologie.com/antholiving / @anthroliving

Article / article.com / @article

Burke Decor / burkedecor.com / @burkedecor

Burrow / burrow.com / @burrow

CB2 / cb2.com / @cb2

The Container Store / containerstore.com / @thecontainerstore

Coterie / coteriebrooklyn.com / @coteriebrooklyn

Crate & Barrel / crateandbarrel.com / @crateandbarrel

France & Son / franceandson.com / @franceandson

H&M Home / ww2.hm.com/en_us / @hmhome

Hawkins NY / hawkinsnewyork.com / @hawkinsnewyork

Industry West / industrywest.com / @industrywest

The Inside / theinside.com / @theinside

Interior Define / interiordefine.com / @interiordefine

Joss & Main / jossandmain.com / @jossandmain

Jungalow / jungalow.com / @thejungalow

Lightology / lightology.com / @lightology

Living Spaces / livingspaces.com / @livingspaces

Lowe's / lowes.com / @loweshomeimprovement

Lulu & Georgia / luluandgeorgia.com / @luluandgeorgia

Minted / minted.com / @minted

The Nopo / thenopo.com / @the.nopo

Overstock / overstock.com / @overstock

Pottery Barn / potterybarn.com / @potterybarn

Rejuvenation / rejuvenation.com / @rejuvenation

Rove Concepts / roveconcepts.com / @roveconcepts

Rug Studio / rugstudio.com / @rugstudio

Serena & Lily / serenaandlily.com / @serenaandlily

Shutterfly / shutterfly.com / @shutterfly

The Sill / thesill.com / @thesill

Society6 / society6.com / @society6

Sundays / sundays-company.com / @sundaysfurniture

Target / target.com / @target

Tempaper & Co. / tempaper.com / @tempaper_designs

Urban Outfitters / urbanoutfitters.com/home / @urbanoutfittershome

Wayfair / wayfair.com / @wayfair

West Elm / westelm.com / @westelm

World Market / worldmarket.com / @worldmarket

Zara Home / zarahome.com / @zarahome

Credits

PHOTOGRAPHERS

ART Furniture: pages 24 (*mirror*), 100, 120–121

Luke Austin: page 72

Bobby Berk wallpaper for Tempaper: pages 25 (Wiggle Room) and 31 (*bottom right*)

Veronica Crawford: pages 21, 32 (*right*), 214, 215, 291 (*top*)

Ashlee Huff: pages 260–261 and 269

iStock: page 25: Chimpinski (*vases*); page 124: chuckcollier; page 242: SuriyaKK (*bottom*)

Karastan: page 99 (*top*)

Sara Ligorria-Tramp: pages 4–5, 5, 8, 12, 16–17, 18, 26–27, 28, 29, 30, 34, 35, 37, 39, 40, 43, 47, 49, 50–51, 52, 56, 58, 59, 60, 66–67, 68, 71, 74, 76–77, 80, 81, 85, 94 (*top left and top right*), 98, 102–103, 104, 112, 113, 114–115, 118, 122, 123, 125, 128–129, 130, 131, 132 (*top*), 133, 140, 144, 146, 147, 149, 156 (*right*), 162, 163, 165, 170, 174–175, 176 (*top left*), 179, 182, 184–185, 188–189, 194–195, 197, 198, 200, 201, 202 (*bottom*), 203 (*bottom*), 204, 206 (*top*), 208, 209, 210 (*left*), 211, 218, 222, 224, 225, 228–229, 230, 231, 233, 235, 238, 239, 244, 252, 256 (*top*), 258–259, 264–265, 266, 274 (*left*), 278, 279, 280, 281, 283, 288, 289, 291 (*middle and bottom*), 293, 294–295

Lulu and Georgia: pages 101 (*top right*) and 167 (*top*)

Marcus Meisler for Molekule: page 167 (*bottom*)

Kara Mercer: pages 15 (*left*), 65 (*bottom left*), 92–93, 101 (*bottom*), 116, 134–135, 150–151, 176 (*bottom right*), 202 (*top*), 210 (*right*), 223 (*top left, bottom left, bottom right*), 234, 240, 242 (*top*), 246–247, 253, 255, 262, 268

Netflix: page 15 (*right*)

Tessa Neustadt: pages 20, 21, 33, 48, 65 (*top left, top right, and bottom right*), 69, 75, 88, 132 (*bottom*), 138, 155, 156 (*left*), 157, 158–159, 160, 161, 166, 173, 180–181, 186, 187, 191, 199, 203 (*top*), 206 (*bottom*), 207, 212–213, 223 (*top right*), 226–227, 236, 243, 248, 256 (*bottom*), 257, 267, 270–271, 272, 274 (*right*), 275, 276, 284

Steven Onoja for Ecco Domani: page 42

Shutterstock: pages 24–25: Pixel-shot (*ottoman*), superbank stock (*plant*), modustollens (*blue pillow*), rdurand (*chair*), Dewin ID (*plate*), AmaPhoto (*sconce*), Dom Toretto (*wood surface*), Akintevs (*wood bowl*), Followtheflow (*leather sofa and side table*), LaMony Betty (*gray sofa*), Igor Kraynov (*terrazzo*), Reiza Fauzy (*black side table*); page 31: glamour (*sweaters*), Akasha (*chunky throw*), fancy (*leather jacket*), nikkimeel (*leather sofa*), inchic (*plaid shirts*); page 32 (*left*): Nublee bin Shamsu Bahar; page 92 (*bottom left*); page 94: Ivelin Denev (*bottom left*) and Alena Ozerova (*bottom right*); page 145: Igisheva Maria (*top left and bottom left*), Kostikova Natalia (*top right*), Pixel-shot (*bottom right*); page 164: j.chizhe; page 176: Didecs (*top right*) and New Africa (*bottom left*); page 177: Sudowoodo (*bathroom sign figures*); page 277: Followtheflow; page 292: mokjc (*top left*), aperturesound (*top center*), Susan Law Cain (*top right*), Rover stock (*middle left*), Rosie Fraser (*middle center*), All for you friend (*middle right*), Dewin ID (*bottom left*), superbank stock (*bottom center*), Homestudio 2 (*bottom right*)

Ivan Solis: pages 2, 99 (*bottom*)

Brady Tolbert: pages 232 (*left*) and 282

Viby Creative: page 153

Marisa Vitale: pages 86, 87, 96, 107 (*bottom*), 108–109, 110, 111, 136, 137, 139, 177, 232 (*right*), 241, 254, 273

Grayson Wilder: pages 23, 168–169, 237

WinWin artlab/Shutterstock: paint swatches on pages 148, 186, 187, 190, 206, 207, 216, 217

INTERIOR DESIGNERS

Alli Tucker Fisher & Justin Fisher, styling by Kate Flynn: page 149

Becca Mendez, the Bam House: page 266

Brady Tolbert: pages 4–5, 12, 21, 28, 29, 32, 37, 47, 52, 85, 118, 123, 132, 133, 156 (*right*), 165, 179 (*right*), 188–189, 222, 232, 235, 279, 282, 283

Caitlin Murray, Black Lacquer Design: page 200

Caryl Waters Style: pages 147 (*left*) and 289 (*right*)

Christine Vroom Interiors: page 68

Grace DeAsis and Julia Rose, Velinda Hellen Design, styling by Emily Bowser: page 278 (*left*)

Jacobschang Architecture, styling by Emily Bowser: page 133 (*top*) and 201 (*bottom*)

Julia Rose, Emily Henderson Design: pages 204 and 281

Linette Dai, SOKO DAI, styling by Emily Bowser: page 130

Real/Nice Design: pages 76–77, 239, 289 (*left*)

Sara Ligorria-Tramp, styling by Emily Bowser: page 112

Tracy Lynn Studio: pages 94 (*top right*) and 291 (*bottom*)

Zachary-Jones Studio: pages 144, 146, 203 (*bottom*), 238

Acknowledgments

We've all heard the quote "it takes a village," and with this book, that was definitely the case. It would not have been possible without the love, care, and support I received from so many wonderful people in my life.

First of all, to my amazing coauthor, Jamie, who painstakingly took all my jumbled-up thoughts, ideas, and stories and put them into a format that is fun, visual, and easy to understand. Jamie understood from our first meeting how important this topic was and gave it all the care it deserved. At the end of the day, she knew that the goal of this book was to help improve the lives of readers by showing them how their home and surroundings can affect and improve their mental wellness and more. Jamie, I couldn't have done it without you. Thank you!

To Kristyn and Esther, my literary goddesses. Thank you for believing in me and my message and helping me get this project out into the world. And to my incredible team at Align PR, who continues to support me in all of my ventures, including my very first book.

To say I would have been lost in this process without the guidance, attention, brilliance, belief (I could go on and on) of the entire Potter team would be an understatement. They couldn't possibly be better partners and I can't thank them enough. Mia, Patricia, Kelli, Chris, Jana, Andrea, and, of course, my editor, Angelin, who helped bring this to life, you are all rock stars and I love you.

I'm so lucky to have such an amazing team at Bobby Berk that has been with me for years and years. I consider each and every one of them to be family, and without their support none of this would be possible. Brady, Sydney, Adam, Awit, Amor, Logan, and Janet: I love you!

My interiors are brought to life and capture what true design does to my soul thanks to the work of brilliant photographers. To Sara, Tessa, Kate, and Marisa— you are simply the best. And to tell a story this detailed requires endless examples of different kinds of spaces, so I want to give a shout-out to the designers who, along with my own work, are also featured in this book. Thank you. Your rooms will never cease to inspire me.

Last and most important, I would like to thank my husband, Dewey, who has stood by my side and supported me for almost twenty years through the good times and the bad and has always believed in me. I love you more than words can express. You are my best friend and my everything.

Index

Published in the United States by Clarkson Potter/Publishers, an imprint of
Random House, a division of Penguin Random House LLC, New York.
ClarksonPotter.com
RandomHouseBooks.com

CLARKSON POTTER is a trademark and POTTER with colophon is a
registered trademark of Penguin Random House LLC.

Library of Congress Cataloging-in-Publication Data
Names: Berk, Bobby, author. | Ligorria-Tramp, Sara, photographer
    (expression) | Neustadt, Tessa, photographer (expression). Title: Right at
    home : how good design is good for the mind / Bobby Berk ; photographs
    by Sara Ligorria-Tramp and Tessa Neustadt. Description: New York :
    Clarkson Potter/Publishers, [2023] | Includes index. Identifiers: LCCN
    2022028620 (print) | LCCN 2022028621 (ebook) | ISBN 9780593578353
    (hardcover) | ISBN 9780593578360 (ebook). Subjects: LCSH: Interior
    decoration—Psychological aspects. Classification: LCC NK2113 .B396
    2023 (print) | LCC NK2113 (ebook) | DDC 747   dc23/eng/20220719
LC record available at https://lccn.loc.gov/2022028620
LC ebook record available at https://lccn.loc.gov/2022028621

ISBN: 978-0-593-57835-3
Ebook ISBN: 978-0-593-57836-0

Printed in China

Bobby Berk Creative Team: Brady Tolbert and Sydney Gilbert
Editor: Angelin Adams
Editorial Assistant: Darian Keels
Designer: Mia Johnson
Design Assistance: Jennifer K. Beal Davis
Illustrator: Andrew Joyce
Production Editor: Patricia Shaw
Production Manager: Kelli Tokos
Compositors: Merri Ann Morrell and Hannah Hunt
Copy Editor: Diana Drew
Indexer: Cathy Dorsey
Marketer: Andrea Portanova
Publicist: Jana Branson

10 9 8 7 6 5 4 3 2 1

First Edition